DOING BUSINESS IN THE EUROPEAN COMMUNITY

Paul Gibbs

KOGAN
PAGE

I thank Ben and Simon because I want to.

First published in 1990 by Kogan Page Ltd
120 Pentonville Road
London N1 9JN.
Reprinted 1990

Editorial packaging: Redfern Publishing Services
Typeset by BookEns, Saffran Walden, Essex
Printed in England by Clays Ltd, St Ives plc

British Library Cataloguing in Publication Data
Gibbs, Paul
   Doing business in the European Community.
   1. European Community countries. Business
   I. Title
   650'.094

ISBN 1-85091-971-2

The Credit Protection Association plc

THE CASH FLOW ENHANCEMENT & COLLECTION SYSTEM FOR EXPORTERS:

All successful businesses are aware that good cash flow is essential to their well-being, whether they are engaged in the home market or in export. This is particularly so during recent periods of very high interest rates. When customers slow down payments to suppliers, the supplier himself either has to delay payment to others or pay for the privilege of borrowing more financing money. Of course, temporary bridging loans or some factoring house can assist with the problem, but these facilities usually prove to be expensive and cumbersome. An original alternative is The Credit Protection Association who have been providing credit management systems since 1914. CPA claim that many hundreds of exporters are already using their services with excellent results. Basically, their system straightforward: they make repeated contact with the customer by letter asking him to settle the overdue account direct. The approaches are psychologically balanced and, as necessary, up to three approaches are made, which usually produce results well in excess of 80%. The letters are despatched in English, French, German or Spanish as desired.

Uniquely, CPA provide members with a minimum performance warranty which will set even the most sceptical potential client at ease.

CPA point out that because of the fear of losing face, many overdue buyers are shy of purchasing further from the supplier until they have discharged their obligation. So, often when they pay through CPA's polite prompting, the way is open to trade again.

CONTENTS

LIST OF FIGURES

LIST OF TABLES

PREFACE

Many books giving information on the European Community exist for businesspeople but few, if any, address the issue of personal interaction with foreign clients in a foreign culture, in the pursuit of business abroad. A potential market of 320 million consumers will, of course, have attractions for all nations. Having a good product or service and good marketing might be sufficient in your home market, but in the European Community many more companies can, and will, claim the same advantages. The choice of business partner will more often than not depend on personal rapport. This book is about creating the right impression, making sure you have a valuable insight into each country's business culture, its behavioural patterns and consumer trends. It will ensure that you do not let avoidable circumstances obstruct your business potential.

Each chapter deals with the process of making and retaining a business contact abroad. The book highlights changes in culture and etiquette, and looks at the different spending habits of consumers throughout the European Community. It also briefly examines the corporate structures of each country's organisations, as well as how to address senior staff, and provides handy tips on conforming to standards of dress.

Being aware of each other's customs and taking the time to prepare yourself for your client's benefit rather than your own will not make a bad product good, nor a good product better, but it will help a good product to be accepted, thus increasing sales and profitability.

Paul Gibbs

ACKNOWLEDGEMENTS

Many people have helped provide information for this book – from trade associations, embassies, financial institutions (especially Touche Ross) and other authorities. I thank them all. In particular, I thank Jane Holliday for her research, editing, typing and enthusiasm.

PART I
PREPARING FOR THE SINGLE EUROPEAN MARKET

INTRODUCTION

Europe is the biggest potential free market to open this century. But, in a sense, it has never been closed. True, national culture, customs and patriotism have constituted both tariff and non-tariff barriers, but very few countries have operated a total boycott which could not in some way have been overcome, given the will. (The Dutch and the Luxembourgers in fact achieved it long before 1992.) However, the unified European market without trade barriers, which will arise after 1992, presents an opportunity for co-operation and competition on an equal footing between countries which has not previously existed. The harmonisation programme will produce a framework more suitable for pan-European initiative, increased efficiency and lower prices, but that will only apply to the few (both large and small) companies that have prepared themselves well.

Those companies which not only take the time to evaluate the special conditions of other foreign markets, but also take time to study customer preferences and business subcultures will stand the best chance of expanding their businesses and maximising their profits in the new Single European Market.

Much has already been written on consumer preference; the oft-quoted example being the key features of the domestic washing machine which appeal to certain nations (front-loaders for the British, controls on the top for Germans and spin lock for the Italians), but little has been written on the different ways of doing business. This book attempts to do this.

Britain, rightly or wrongly, has often been considered the 'odd country out', vetoing rather than agreeing. So before exploring the detail country by country, how does one particular EC member's infrastructure (namely the UK) stand up to examination when compared with other major European Community countries? The conclusion is, unfortunately, not well. In a survey carried out by a leading management accountancy firm, the four European countries geographically nearest to Britain were compared on a range of criteria: location, internationalism, efficiency and reliability. On a ranking system where 1 represents the best and 5 the worst, they scored as follows:

Table A   Five EC countries infrastructure scoring

| | Number of Scores | |
	Highest	Lowest
Great Britain	4	10
France	1	4
Germany	2	7
Netherlands	15	0
Belgium	4	4

Clearly, Britain has by no means a natural lead in doing business in Europe, nor is there any advantage for countries to choose Britain as the route through which to do such business.

Table B   Infrastructure ratings of five EC countries

	Ranking	1	2	3	4	5
Location:	airport	NL	GB	D	F	B
	road transport	NL	D	B	F	GB
Local characteristics:						
international:	secondary schooling	B	NL	F	GB	D
	higher education	NL	D	B	F	GB
	mastery of foreign languages	NL	B	D	F	GB
	export quotes of GDP	B	NL	D	GB	F
	direct investment abroad	NL	GB	F	D	B
	product acceptance abroad	NL	D	B	GB	F
efficient:	rental value offices	NL	B	D	F	GB
	rental value industrial	NL	B	D	F	GB
	building cost offices	B	F	NL	D	GB
	building cost industrial	NL	B	F	D	GB
	value added per labour unit	F	NL	D	GB	B
	wage increases/ common currency	GB	F	NL	B	D

Ranking:	1	2	3	4	5
real interest rates	D	F	NL	GB	B
total tele-communications	GB	NL	F	B	D
digital leased circuits	NL	F	B	GB	D
average pay, chief executives	B	NL	GB	F	D
cost of living	NL	B	D	GB	F
corporate tax rates, small companies	GB	B	NL	F	D
corporate tax rates, larger companies	GB	NL	F	B	D
ROI US companies all industries	NL	B	F	D	GB
ROI US companies manufacturing	D	F	NL	B	GB
reliable: stability of a country	NL	D	GB	B	F
way labour affects companies	NL	D	B	F	GB
working days lost in industry	NL	D	F	GB	—

Missing from this list is a country's political will to be European. The illogical state of affairs that is the core of the British Government's stance on the issue of the European Monetary System (EMS) seems more political than economic. This political stance was made clear in the summer of 1988 at the Brussels Summit Meeting but blurred later at Madrid. Ministers are now instructed to oppose in Brussels anything that could be interpreted as an arrogation by the Community of national sovereignty. This has lead to the absurdity of Britain spurning European money for foreign language teaching. The public announcements by Messrs Heath and Heseltine in support of greater European unity contrast sharply with the Prime Minister's concern for the growth of a social Europe.

EUROPEAN ELECTIONS

Simultaneous (or almost simultaneous) elections for all member states for membership of the European Parliament have been the norm since 1979. Each country uses its own system which, with the exception of the UK, gives some form of proportional representation. The elections of 15 June 1989 took place in Ireland, Denmark, Spain and the UK (proportional represent-ation in Northern Ireland). The Netherlands, France, Germany, Italy, Belgium, Greece and Luxembourg voted on 18 June 1989.

The electoral systems used for the elections were as follows:

Belgium	Proportional representation by lists. The seats are split 13 for Flemish-speaking areas, 11 for the French- and German-speaking. Voters can cast votes for an entire party list or for individual candidates. Total member-ship 16.
	Percentage voting: 1984 92.2 per cent; 1989 90.7 per cent
Denmark	Proportional representation by list. Votes can be cast for an entire party or individual candidates. Total membership 16.
	Percentage voting: 1984 52.5 per cent; 1989 46.2 per cent
France	Proportional representation by party lists. Each party puts forward a national list of candidates who are elected in proportion to the party's national share at the vote. Parties with less than 5 per cent are excluded. Total membership 81.
	Percentage voting: 1984 56.7 per cent; 1989 48.7 per cent
Greece	Proportional representation by party list. Total membership 24.
	Percentage voting: 1984 77.2 per cent; 1989 79.9 per cent
Ireland	Single transferable votes in four constitu-encies. Total membership 15.
	Percentage voting: 1984 47.6 per cent; 1989 68.3 per cent
Italy	Proportional representation by party lists in five regional constituencies and voters choose both party and individual candidates. Seats are allocated to the parties' share of the votes at regional level. Total membership 81.
	Percentage voting: 1984 83.9 per cent; 1989 81.0 per cent
Luxembourg	Proportional representation by lists. Total membership 6.
	Percentage voting: 1984 82 per cent; 1989 87.4 per cent
The Netherlands	Proportional representation by lists and seats

are allocated by share of the vote at national level. Total membership 25.
Percentage voting: 1984 50.5 per cent; 1989 47.2 per cent

Portugal
Proportional representation by lists. Total membership 24.
Percentage voting: 1986 72.7 per cent; 1989 51.2 per cent

Spain
Proportional representation by lists and seats allocated by share of the vote at national level. Total membership 60.
Percentage voting: 1986 68.9 per cent; 1989 54.8 per cent

UK
Individual elections in 78 single member constituencies in the UK; in Northern Ireland, single transferable vote in a single constituency covering the whole of the country. Three MEPs elected. Total membership 81.
Percentage voting: 1984 UK 32.6 per cent, NI 47.6 per cent; 1989 UK 36.2 per cent, NI 47.7 per cent

West Germany
Proportional representation by party lists put forward at national or regional level. Candidates are elected in proportion to the party's share of the vote. Total membership 81.
Percentage voting: 1984 56.8 per cent; 1989 62.3 per cent

The political shape of the Parliament and the mandate it has to take Europe into a new, barrier-free society impacts on business decisions. The most significant trend of the 1989 elections has been the move towards a more socialist Parliament and an environmentally-aware electorate. This trend in voting mirrors the trends referred to later in this book under 'Consumer Trends'.

This book does not intend to offer answers to the political and sovereignty issues. Rather, it is addressed to those who are going to do business in the European Community and who may need some help.

The first three chapters deal with the background to the community's development, the essence of international marketing, and pointers to understanding behaviours of a non-verbal character within member states. Then each country is addressed in a fairly consistent manner, although an exact format approach has been avoided in order to allow individual country differences to emerge. (For instance, there is greater emphasis on eating in Spain and rather less in the Netherlands.) The last part of each chapter deals with setting up a business in the country, its management structure, information on letter writing and marketing infrastructure.

Of course, no individual is exactly the same as another, nor can any nation be more than a focused unit of individuals, but gross differences can generally be observed and some of these, where they impact on business transactions, are reported here. Not all apply in all circumstances, but they do give a pointer, at the very least, as to what to expect.

If any overriding business behaviours emerge throughout the book, they may be summarised as:

- Be polite; very polite.
- Be prepared; very prepared.
- Be patient; very – well, enough to trade off time spent and potential reward.

I
INTERNATIONAL MARKETING

The dismantling of psychological and geographical barriers to the purchase of your goods can only be assisted by the harmonisation of the standards, working practices and monetary union within the Single Market. And it can only be achieved with strong international marketing skills which include: identifying international marketing opportunities, analysing the chosen geographic market's infrastructure and then deciding upon an entry strategy. Having successfully completed these, it is necessary to assess the impact of international markets upon price, distribution and the logistical problem of manufacture and delivery, the promotion of the product in an international environment and, finally, the centralised or decentralised control of a multinational marketing operation must be faced and resolved.

WHY GO ABROAD?

Generally, the reasons for even considering an international expansion of a company's activities fall into four separate areas: **1.** market size (leading to product effectiveness and competitive edge); **2.** external influences (economic healthiness or less intense competition than home markets); **3.** geographical diversification (in place of product range extension or business diversification); and **4.** product longevity (where international sales of a product would make that product's trading cycle more robust).

This seems a very logical approach, and is certainly one which the 1992 focus encourages. However, it is important to remember that by far the easiest way of promoting business growth is through the expansion of existing markets. In coming to the conclusion that Europe may offer exciting opportunities for your business, do ensure that you are not ignoring the possibilities of your own home market.

Given that international diversification makes sound sense, and your existing market position is secure, how do you go about selecting the appropriate country? All markets are dynamic and react to their own particular mixture of socio-cultural, political, legal and governmental traits. Understanding the direction and the stability of these 'environments' are just as important, as they either relate to consumer choice or they affect the logistical decisions regarding distribution, manufacturing and promotion.

Awareness of social and cultural norms has helped major multinational companies such as Coca Cola, IBM, Marlborough and Pepsi succeed in being recognised as truly international brands. It also helps the British salesman to understand the prejudices with which he is met and enables him to overcome them. In a recent study of Swedish, Italian, French and German buyers of heavy engineering products, the following stereotyping of the British emerged:

- low productivity;
- non-competitive pricing strategies;
- poor and unresponsive product design;
- poor marketing.

It is indeed surprising that Britain has any heavy engineering products at all!

The cultural tapestry of many foreign countries (including Europe) is unavailable to British businessmen because of language barriers. Little or no mastery of the language leaves an understanding of a country to third-hand interpretation. The tonal shades of the aesthetic qualities of community life are lost and with them the depth of relationship which facilitates serious business transactions.

Table 1.1 Percentage of adults speaking European languages

	Belg	Den	Fra	Ger	Ire	It	Neth	Sp	UK
	%	%	%	%	%	%	%	%	%
English	26	51	26	43	99	13	68	13	100
French	71	5	100	18	12	27	31	15	15
German	22	48	11	100	2	6	67	3	6
Italian	4	1	8	3	1	100	2	4	1
Spanish	3	1	13	1	1	5	4	100	2
Flemish/Dutch	68	1	1	3	—	—	100	—	1

Note   No figures available for Portugal, Greece or Luxembourg
Source   G/AA

Economic analysis, however, is generally available from many sources, and enables gross and objective evaluation of a market's potential. Of critical importance in any review are the trading practices of the country or countries concerned. Although General Agreement of Trade Tariffs (GATT) has done much to reduce tariff barriers throughout the world, it has not done (and nor could it do) much to reduce the importance of non-tariff barriers such as chauvinism (eg the Australian 'buy Australian and be proud' campaign).

Some headway has been made towards the goal of a free market, but the EC itself is not without its own hypocritical interpretations. The EC has regulated against dumping its goods on its internal states, but does not stop at dumping butter, for instance, on the Soviet Union. The EC has paticular anti-dumping measures regarding steel, textiles and heavy engineering equipment. The French have their own way of dealing with the problem, whether it be British lamb or Japanese video cassettes. The French psyche can construct such complications that it becomes impossible actively to develop the market.

Political risk is also a key area of the evaluation. Although the EC does not suffer the extravagant and violent swings of fundamentalist Moslem states or the overt corruption of Latin America, nevertheless, the damage caused by changing personal tax rates, politically-driven currency valuations or nationalisation policies can ruin business plans designed upon a stable political environment. Political risk assessment techniques have been developed at the University of Delaware. It ranks each selected country on 15 economic, political and financial factors and gives the country a rating between zero and one hundred.

Finally, consumer data. Although standardisation has become more common, a universal quantitative measure which can give meaningful pan-European relative comparisons has not yet been found. Measurements such as the percentage of the population with a university education may give some insight, but many indirect UK measurements are so open to distortion that they become no more than broad brush pointers when applied to many European countries. To test consumer reaction to any product proposition requires a local visit.

However, before such a visit, much information can be collected from the Department of Trade and Industry, the British Overseas Trade Board, the Commission of the European Communities, the European Investment Bank, the United Nations Commission for Europe, banks, investment houses, trade associations and Chambers of Commerce.

Having undertaken a wide-ranging international study (grants are available from the DTI) and having made a decision on the appropriateness of a marketing venture, the entry strategy has to be considered. In essence, there are five ways in which products can be sold to foreign consumers:

1. Through agents (UK embassies and foreign trade associations can help in selection).
2. Through external distributors (sole distributors of products acting as principals).
3. Through external management control on indigenous enterprises (for example, Hilton Hotels).
4. Through franchising (for example, Benetton).
5. Through licensing (for example, Mickey Mouse).

Each of these has specific advantages and weaknesses and suits distinct types of business at different states of their international marketing development. The following table highlights the cost of entry with the expected climate for new international ventures.

Table 1.2   Entry strategy guide

WELCOMING INVESTMENT CLIMATE

C O S T O F E N T R Y		HIGH	MEDIUM	LOW
	HIGH	Wholly owned joint venture	Assembly	Franchising
	MEDIUM	Joint equity venture	Industrial co-operation	Know-how, contracts
	LOW	Sales	Management contracts	Exporting

Source   Stanley J. Paliwoda, *International Marketing*

It is obvious, therefore, that highly-committed companies are likely to receive the best host support, because not only do they create economic wealth within the country directly related to the product but also through companies servicing them. But the cost is high and so is the risk. To balance that, the managment product-to-sales chain is more under control, marketing knowledge is more extensive and appropriate long-term objectives more realisable. Certainly, the cost of exporting to a country and using agents would seem, on the surface, a lower risk, but with little or no actual control over the promotion of your product, spurious management information can be generated, which makes expansion decisions very much harder.

It is unlikely that the product being offered exactly matches the new market's needs, although this should be less of a Community problem post-1992. The product policy decisions themselves fall into two groups: product modification and standardisation. McDonald's, 7-Up, Benetton, International Traveller hotels and 'high net worth' banking have all taken the route of seeking product economies of scale and reduction in development costs. Larger budgets, uncomplicated products and actual market segmentation can create receptive markets.

Other product categories may not be so lucky. Modifications can be necessitated by legal requirements, tariffs, nationalism, technical requirements, taxation, climate and, of course, consumer tastes.

The costs of matching these manifest and hidden restrictions need to be understood and incorporated into the pricing of the product. Alcoholic drinks tailor both their strength and image to fit local markets. Obvious pricing elements contribute to the competitive edge of the product, such as local worker pay rates, accommodation, exchange controls, currency invoicing and other export overheads. Each of these will influence which cell in the entry strategy guide should be used.

THE PROMOTION OF GLOBAL PRODUCTS

There are few, if any, truly global products that take on a 'personality' or status which enhances the consumer's use or consumption, for which (usually) he is prepared to pay a premium. As the following table shows, there is great variation in the ranking of brands across the three major world economies. The figures come from a study produced by Landor Associates of 1,000 consumers in each market. Equal weighting was given to customer familiarity with each name and their 'esteem' for it. For instance, Coca Cola was ranked first in Europe for familiarity, but sixty-sixth in esteem: it finished sixth overall.

Only sound investigation into all of the many elements of an international promotion campaign will give it the best chance of success. Public relations, packaging, sales promotion, advertising and direct response must all be carefully considered. For instance, direct response may seem a good idea, but what about postal regulations, currency instability? And how about the product name? Will it travel? Take the examples of SIC and

Table 1.3   World-wide brand rankings

	Ranking in: Europe	US	Japan
1 Coca Cola	6	1	2
2 IBM	24	51	8
3 Sony	16	68	4
4 Porsche	5	73	22
5 McDonald's	78	5	26
6 Disney	52	11	53
7 Honda	29	62	37
8 Toyota	64	64	6
9 Seiko	47	91	10
10 BMW	8	71	96
11 Volkswagen	3	112	72
12 Mercedes	1	37	151

PSCHITT (two French soft drinks), BUM (a Spanish potato chip) and SUPER PISS (a Finnish product for unfreezing car door locks). Less obvious is the pronunciation factor; for example, the pronunciation of Park Lane cigarettes causes difficulties for speakers of the Spanish language, thus sales are bound to be slow.

2
1992 – THE STORY SO FAR

By 1992, the 12 countries of the European Community will seek to have a free trade union which, in theory, should enhance the economic and social lives of over 320 million people that make up its population. This economic power, a GDP greater than the USA and over 250 per cent of the world average, and about one-third of the world's exports, should position it as the third major player in world affairs alongside the USA and Japan (rapidly growing in political as well as economic influence).

Such strength will, however, require goodwill on behalf of the Community's national governments, as well as a change in the cultural perceptions of the individual countries. Andrew Shenfield, in a BBC Reith Lecture in 1972, described the Community thus:

'It is more like a bag of marbles than a melting-pot, the marbles are soft on the surface and made of some sticky substance, like putty, which keeps them clinging together as they are pushed around and constantly make contact with one another in the bag. It does not sound very attractive; it certainly is not very coherent. It is much less satisfactory to describe than the simplified version of a supranational European government which was the ideal of the founding fathers of the community.'

Be that as it may, the Community has enlarged itself and dealt with some of the urgent problems created by the Common Agricultural Policy. Britain, a member since 1 January 1973, has, and currently is, finding its European feet. France, always, it seems, suspicious of British intentions and full of self-importance as a founder member, is again locked in an ideological battle over sovereignty and the European Company status. However, it is not intended to discuss Community political anomalies here.

HISTORICAL BACKGROUND

The growth of a European federation is certainly not a new idea, even given its modern-day stimulus from the atrocities of the Second World War and a desire to keep the peace between France and West Germany. As early as the fourteenth century, Pierre Dubois proposed a European Confederation to be governed by a European Council. Britain's own William Penn in 1693 suggested a European Parliament as a means of securing a peaceful Europe. But it was the close of the Second World War and the ensuing economic, defensive and political needs that were the catalysts which led to the signing by six countries – France, West Germany, Italy, the Netherlands, Belgium and Luxembourg – of the Treaty of Rome on 25 March 1957 and the creation of the EEC on 1 January 1958.

The original agreement committed the six countries to a far-reaching exercise of economic integration over a 12-year period. Between 1958 and 1969, the 'six' created the kind of economic community envisaged in the Rome treaty. The basic elements of customs union, internal tariff and quota dismantlement, and the construction of the common external tariff were established ahead of schedule. Non-tariff barriers were attacked, the Common Agricultural Policy was operational and trade and arrangements with colonial dependencies were devised.

Britain had participated in early discussions but, for many reasons, joined Norway, Sweden, Denmark, Austria, Switzerland and Portugal in establishing the European Free Trade Association. She quickly recognised, however, that the EEC was the route most likely to fulfil her aims.

Thus in 1961 Britain applied for full membership of the EEC. Negotiations were, however, abruptly terminated in 1963, as were the applications for fellow EFTA countries Norway and Denmark, and a separate application by the Republic of Ireland. New negotiations began in 1969 which ultimately led, through a more committed and sensitive approach by the British Government, to membership on 1 January 1973. All four nations were accepted, but Norway, after a national referendum, declined membership. Britain renegotiated its terms in 1975 and, having put these to a national referendum, gained overwhelming support to retain its membership.

The second enlargement of the Community came with the membership of Greece and the Iberian countries of Spain and Portugal. Trading ties between these countries and the Community were in place long before their full membership of the Community. The turning point seemed to be the return of democracy in these countries. Their election to membership in all but political terms weakened the union, increased the population base by one-fifth and the GNP by one-tenth. Membership came first to Greece on 1 January 1981, and then to Portugal and Spain on 1 January 1986. All three have underdeveloped economies and have been given an extended period to conform with the directives of the Community.

The most significant event on the road to securing European union since the Treaty of Rome is the Single European Act. In 1985 the heads of state agreed to a programme comprising 300 separate pieces of legislation. To facilitate the enactment of these, the Luxembourg Summit of 1985 adopted several proposals prepared to create a European union and then, in February 1986, the Single European Act. The Act replaces the unanimity required for any enactment of Community legislation. It permits decisions to be made by a qualifying majority of ministers with regard to measures which have the establishing and functioning of the internal market as their principal objective.

The Act covers a broad spectrum and such diverse areas as: economic and social cohesion, environment, co-operation between institutions, and political co-operation. The adoption of the Act stopped the practice of travelling at the pace of the slowest dissenting member and shows a political will to dispense with the inefficiencies of fragmentation and so provides a unified market.

THE DECISION-MAKING BODIES

The main decision-making bodies of the Community are: the Commission; the Council of Ministers; the Court of Justice; the Parliamentary Assembly; and the Economic and Social Committee. In addition, there are said to be 2,000 committees, subcommittees and working parties.

The Commission

Commissioners are appointed by the member governments for four-year renewable terms, and are resident in Brussels. The main duty with which they are entrusted is to make proposals for Community action to the Council of Ministers. The President and Vice-President are chosen from amongst the 14 Commissioners and hold their offices for two-year renewable terms. The UK, West Germany, France and Italy each nominated two Commissioners, whilst the smaller states, Belgium, the Netherlands, Ireland, Denmark and Luxembourg, nominated one each. Spain is to nominate two, and Portugal and Greece one each. *maybe*

Each Commissioner is responsible for a portfolio, although some will carry more than one portfolio. Each has a private office (cabinet) to which he makes the appointments. Invariably, the members appointed are of the same nationality as the Commissioner. His deputy is known as the *chef du cabinet*. Beneath the Commissioner, there will be one or more Director General – similar to the permanent head of a ministry – who is responsible for a broad policy area, and he will, in turn, have below him Directors and Heads of Division.

The need for Commissioners to be impartial at all times is enshrined in the Treaty of Rome (Article 157) which requires that Commissioners 'shall neither seek nor take instruction from any Government or from any other body'. However, as the Commission only employs 11,000 staff (including translators, interpreters and some 2,600 in the separate scientific and technological Joint Research Centre) – as against perhaps 20,000 for a British Ministry – it is not hard to see that the Commission can only hope to be effective if the governmental departments of its member states agree to administer its policies. If the Commissioners approve of the draft directive drawn up by a Directorate-General, after any necessary amendments, it is then proposed by the Commission as a draft directive to the Council of Ministers. This gives member states, through the Council of Ministers, the final say on whether the directive becomes law or not. It can, however, take years before legislation is accepted and becomes law.

The Council of Ministers

The Council of Ministers consists of a minister from each member-state government, and the ministers change according to the subjects on the agenda. Ministers represent the interests of their own governments, but try to arrive at agreements which are in the Community's interest. There is a system of qualified voting so that France, West Germany, Italy and the UK have ten votes each; the Netherlands, Belgium and Greece five votes; Ireland and Denmark three; and Luxembourg two. For a qualified majority, 45 votes are required, but when the Council votes on a proposal that does not emanate from the Commission, then, in addition, the support of six states is also necessary. The Council of Ministers meets only for a certain number of days in the year, and is not resident in Brussels. Each member state takes a six-month turn to chair Council meetings, a national minister of foreign affairs being President of the Council during that period. There is a small permanent staff in Brussels, but the main preparatory work is undertaken by the ambassadors and their embassy staff.

The ambassadors or representatives act as a link between the member countries and the Community. They meet in the

Committee of Permanent Representatives (known as COREPER), prepare agenda and agree non-contentious proposals, so that when the ministers attend much has already been agreed and only matters still in dispute need to be negotiated.

The European Council is a meeting of 'the heads of state and government' although, in fact, the only head of state who attends is the president of France, the other countries being represented by their prime ministers. It takes place twice a year and contentious issues which have not been resolved at the Council of Ministers are discussed in the European Council. It is the heads of government who have the authority not only to impose unpopular decisions but also to convince their opposing political forces in their own countries of the need for such decisions. At the end of each Council a communique is issued, giving the broad outline of what has been agreed.

The Court of Justice

The Court of Justice is the ultimate interpreter of the treaties on which the EC is based and the final arbiter of disputes concerning secondary legislation whenever there is a query or disagreement about the meaning of a particular regulation, directive or decision. It is situated in Luxembourg with a staff of 460. There are 11 judges, each appointed for six years. Hearings are in public, but deliberations are private. A judge can only be removed by the unanimous vote of his colleagues to the effect that he is no longer capable of carrying out his duties. A quorum consists of seven judges; there must be an odd number sitting and decisions are reached by simple majority. The Court produces its own reports containing the basic facts of the case, the summing up by the Advocate-General and the judgement. Companies on whom the Commission has imposed fines may appeal to the Court. The Court also gives preliminary rulings for the benefit of national courts. It may proceed against member states if a member state is not fulfilling its legal obligations. It reviews the legality of Community acts and it settles disputes.

The Parliamentary Assembly

Until 1981 the European Parliament held one-third of its sessions in Luxembourg and two-thirds in Strasbourg, in Eastern France. In 1981 it decided to hold no more sessions in Luxembourg, and this was upheld by the Court of Justice. However, more than three-quarters of the parliamentary secretariat of approximately 2,600 are based in Luxembourg which means that they have to travel between the two points regularly.

The first direct elections to the European Parliament were

THE CO-OPERATION PROCEDURE

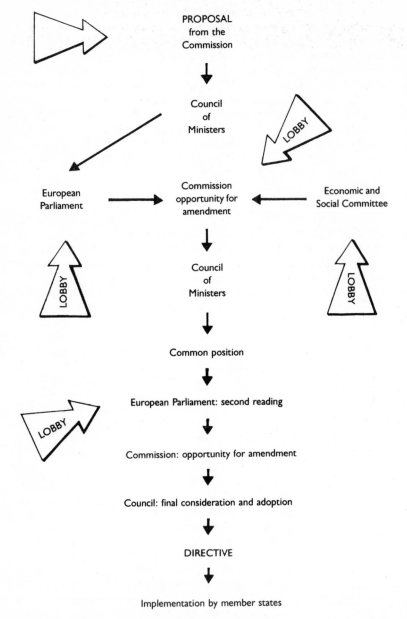

Figure 1 The enactment of an EC Directive

held in June 1979. There are 434 members of the European Parliament who control 15 important committees which scrutinise Commission proposals and prepare reports. They have the right to dismiss the government, ie the Commissioners, provided over half the members vote in favour of this. They also have the final vote on a part of the European Community's budget allocation, and can reject the budget as a whole. They give an opinion, which is not binding, on European laws sent from the Commission to the Council of Ministers.

The Economic and Social Committee

The Economic and Social Committee is purely consultative. Its membership is appointed for four years and currently numbers 156: for example, 24 from France, West Germany and the UK; 12 from Belgium and the Netherlands; 9 from Denmark and Ireland; and 6 from Luxembourg. The spectrum of its membership is broad and includes producers, workers, farmers, transport operators, merchants; as well as personnel from the professions, universities, consumer organisations and other appropriate interest groups. Its members are selected by the Council from lists submitted by member states. No particular importance is assigned to its role. Its functions are more akin to an in-house opinion poll for the Council and Commission. Its decisions are reached in open debate in full sessions, rather than by lobbying.

THE LEGAL PROCESSES

Although the Community's infrastructure is now able to cope with the political intent and the workload required to achieve the 1992 objectives, just under half of the proposed legislative measures put forward by the European Commission have been adopted by the Council of Ministers. It is still possible to influence the outcome of the laws, to lobby for a particular cause or to seek redress where unfair barriers to trade still remain. For this an understanding of the legal process is necessary.

Basically, the legal process consists of four main procedures:

1. The Commission drafts a proposal which it submits to the Council.
2. The Parliament and the Economic and Social Committee (ECOSOC) consider the proposal and formulate an opinion. Amendment may be required by the Commission.
3. The Council of Ministers, taking the opinions of the Parliament and ECOSOC into account, formulate a common position and the proposal is returned to the Parliament for a second reading.

4. If the Parliament agrees with the Council, then it may adopt the proposal by qualified majority voting.

This is known as the Co-operation Procedure and was made possible by the Single European Act. Before that, the Council of Ministers considered proposals which were then adopted by unanimity or not at all.

There are four different sorts of legislative meaures:

1. *Regulations,* which are laws binding on all member states. They can be adopted by the Council of Ministers and the Commission. No national laws are required.
2. *Directives,* which define the end result, but allow each nation to introduce its own legislation to achieve the goal.
3. *Decisions,* which are similar to regulations and are binding on whom they address.
4. *Recommendations,* which are not law, and therefore not binding.

Pre-lobbying

Lobbying can be conducted at all stages of the legislative process. Obviously, the first step is to lobby at the Commission before draft proposals are produced. The Department of Trade and Industry (DTI) (UK) is prepared to release the names of civil servants who can help in certain areas. Lobbying organisations or trade associations can help with direct lobbying.

As in Britain, lobbying can be done through members of the European Parliament, or representation may be made to the other consultative organ, the Economic and Social Committee. The other route, albeit rather closer to the actual decision, is the Committee of Permanent Representatives, where the working parties for the Council of Ministers are formed to review the Council proposals.

Post-lobbying

The DTI have produced a booklet entitled *The Single Market: Europe Open for Business* which describes the criteria for making a complaint that the Community rules are working unfairly. It comments:

'The European Court of Justice has also laid down broad guidelines that any rules enacted by member states which are capable of hindering, directly or indirectly, actually or potentially, intra-community trade are covered by Article 30 (establishing the principle that member states cannot maintain quantitative restrictions, or measures which have the equivalent effect, on products from other member states). The measures prohibited include any discrimination between home produced and foreign goods, onerous technical standards or testing procedures, burdensome labelling requirements, unequal taxation regimes, over-rigid pricing or profit margin controls, requirements for import licences or similar procedures, and many other obstacles.'

The DTI is prepared to take up cases of unfair barriers to trade where UK firms face them in other member states. It will also give advice for companies facing what they believe to be unfair trading practices.

USEFUL ADDRESSES

Lobbying (pre-)
Department of Trade and Industry
1–19 Victoria Street
London SW1H OET
Tel: The DTI Hotline 01-200 1992

Unfair practices
Internal European Policy Division
Department of Trade and Industry
Room 405
1–19 Victoria Street
London SW1H OET
Tel: 01-215 4703

General information on EC matters can be obtained from the Commission's UK offices:

8 Storey's Gate
London SW1P 3AT
Tel: 01-222 8122

Windsor House
9–15 Bedford Street
Belfast BT2 7EG
Tel: 0232 40708

4 Cathedral Road
Cardiff CF1 9JG
Tel: 0222 371631

7 Alva Street
Edinburgh EH2 4PH
Tel: 041-225 2058

Information about the European Parliament may be obtained from:

The European Parliament Information Office
2 Queen Anne's Gate
London SW1H 9AA
Tel: 01-222 0411

Information on Centres for European Business Information, including Small and Medium Enterprises Task Force may be obtained from:

Centre for European Business Information
Small Firms Service
2–18 Ebury Bridge Road
London SW1W 8QD
Tel: 01-730 8155

Birmingham Chamber of Industry and Commerce
75 Harborne Road
Birmingham B15 3DH
Tel: 021-454 6171

Newcastle Polytechnic Library
Ellison Building
Ellison Place
Newcastle-upon-Tyne NE1 8ST
Tel: 091-232 6002

Strathclyde Euro Info Centre
25 Bothwell Street
Glasgow G2 6NR
Tel: 041-221 0999

3
MARKETING OPPORTUNITIES IN A UNITED EUROPE

The specifics of international marketing will apply equally well to the harmonised European Community post-1992. The cultural and social influences will remain prominent, but the problems and inefficiencies of excessive red tape should disappear; closed public procurement will be finished and a plethora of other product regulations will be standardised.

The completion of the European internal market should achieve one main objective: significant reduction in costs to the consumer. This will be achieved in three main ways:

1. Through economies of scale in product, and businesses rationalising their own organisations.
2. The more open market competitiveness will result in a greater requirement to achieve and retain market share.
3. There will be increased innovation to match consumer needs. As technology itself responds to the free-market atmosphere, consumer-oriented marketing strategies will be the order of the day. Those unable to react will fail.

Potential price falls to the consumers' advantage cover a wide range of products and services. For instance, pharmaceutical prices could fall by 52 per cent in Germany, 40 per cent in the UK; office machine instrumentation could produce a 27 per cent saving in Italy; telephones a 20 per cent saving in Belgium; financial services 34 per cent in Spain and 23 per cent in Belgium.

Companies themselves can look forward to healthier profits for the following reasons:

- lower input costs;
- responsiveness to profit through:
  (a) utilisation of production capacity
  (b) the use of best practice production techniques;
- removal of non-tariff barriers;
- cross-frontier research and development.

The successful company will be an efficient company and will enjoy the profit rewards even when prices fall. Paolo Cecchini, in his influential study *The Benefits of a Single Market* concluded: 'EC market integration heralds a prospect of rich pickings to be earned, not inherited.'

WHICH INDUSTRIES STAND TO WIN?

A recent study by Ernst & Whinney (now Ernst & Young) and The Industrial Society identified industrial sectors which are most likely to be affected by the drive to European standardisation and market cohesion, and which stand to benefit. In addition, financial services, through the prestige of London, are still (after the crash of 1987) well placed.

1. High technology and telecommunications

Due to the fragmented nature of this industry, much can be gained by inter-operability and compatibility of systems and charges. For instance, as all restrictions on the value of goods that can be sent through the post between EC countries will be scrapped, there could be a boom in mail order. The expansion, if it occurs, will depend on the harmonisation of VAT and the scrapping of customs handling charges. La Redoute, a major French mailing house, familiar with British tastes through its printing of catalogues in English markets in Gibraltar, Malta and the Middle East, is hedging its bets and has already bought a valuable foothold in the UK market through a 25 per cent stake in Empire Stores.

A major debate about the future of telecommunications in Europe was prompted by a *Green Paper* published by the Commission in June 1987. This Paper envisaged full liberalisation of the market for terminal equipment: accelerated work on common standards; complete separation of postal and telecommunications authorities regulatory and operational functions; a free market in value-added services by allowing service providers free access to networks in other member states; full application of the competition provisions of the EEC Treaty to telecommunications; greater emphasis on Europewide services through rapid implementation of the RACE programme, the co-ordinated introduction of the Integrated Services Digital Network and the full application of public pan-European cellular digital mobile communications; and a liberalised environment for point-to-point satellite telecommunications.

Intensive work is under way towards achieving these objectives and there is every possibility that by 1992 a vast market for integrated services will have been opened up in a way which was not previously possible.

2. Pharmaceuticals and chemicals

The Commission seeks to develop a single market in the following ways:

- by imposing a multi-state application procedure for drug licensing;
- by harmonising drug testing, licensing, packaging and pricing;
- by limiting the marketing of dangerous goods.

The EC has developed a series of directives, the main purpose of which has always remained the protection of public health. They lay down criteria for judging the efficiency, quality and safety of medical products and have established a forum for discussion on problems of common interest. They have also facilitated more rapid technological development by encouraging member states to work together on the evaluation of new, high technology products.

Companies can now apply for marketing authorisation in a number of member states at the same time instead of submitting separate applications to individual licensing authorities, although each national authority retains the right to decide for itself whether or not the product should be authorised. The Commission also intends to make further proposals to reduce price barriers, thus stimulating free trade while taking account of the need to encourage the future development of an innovative pharmaceutical industry.

The opening up of non-national contracts from public authorities, including publicity, finance and health, should lead to pan-European sales and marketing and, because of the size of the market, faster recoupment of research and development costs. In the single market, price variations should be narrowed (Zyloric, a drug to reduce the body's retention of uric acid, costs ten times more in Ireland than it does in Spain), and savings for state health-care authorities could average around 3 per cent.

3. Food and drink

Harmonisation of all the pre-and post-manufacturing functions should have considerable impact in creating opportunities to increase or develop pan-European branding, packaging and marketing. But there is little fear of 'EUROFIZZ beer' and 'EUROSAUSAGES'. The European Commission Court of Justice has ruled that any food product legally sold in one common market country has the automatic right to be sold in any other, unless it can be objectively proved that the product is harmful to health. Individual countries can still impose standards on their own manufacturers, such as beer purity laws and Italian pasta specifications, but these cannot be used to bar imports from other Community countries.

The existing and proposed Commission directives on food and drink are quite complex, and have proved very difficult to agree between the parties. It is unlikely, therefore, that the EC will introduce further detailed requirements for products not already covered. Instead, the EC's food harmonisation programme concentrates on establishing a more informative system of food labelling and on setting general food safety and hygiene standards. This should ensure that the Euro-consumer is well informed about the food he or she is buying and can rely on the quality of goods, regardless of the country of origin.

The alcoholic drinks sector will also be affected by changes not only in manufacturing but also in the harmonisation of VAT and excise duties. In Britain, drinks prices in off-licences and supermarkets should drop below existing levels, and some will be even lower than current prices in duty-free shops at airports. At present, Scotch whisky is cheaper in some Community countries than in Scotland.

4. Manufacturing

The main impact will be on inefficient manufacturers protected by nationalistic practices, who will face increased competition. Those who are efficient should benefit from economies of scale, Euro-wide research and development, improved competitiveness in tendering for public procurement contracts and European stock management.

The most significant 1992 legislation concerns:

- harmonisation of technical standards and specifications;
- reduction in restrictive public procurement practices in telecommunications, pharmaceuticals, energy, transport and water sectors;
- approximation of indirect tax;
- limitation of state funding for national industries.

For instance, VAT charged on children's clothing is zero in Britain, but 18.6 per cent in France (the Community has a 0–38 per cent range for VAT). The Commission wishes to standardises this rate. The single market should allow more British clothes to be sold in member states and, of course, more clothes to be sold in the UK. Increased competition will encourage better quality and style, and lower prices.

5. Transport

Following the liberalisation of central transport policy, the move to 1992 concentrates on the liberalisation of transport within member states. Fundamentally this will entail:

- access to new markets, and cabotage limitations being phased out;
- reduced documentation and delays for road hauliers (although a simplified single custom document already exists, it is so detailed that errors can lead to hauliers being turned back at customs);
- increased competition, particularly in air services and fares;
- introduction of a modern shipping policy.

Numerous directives have already been implemented covering shipping, civil aviation, road haulage, road passenger transport and railways. Liberalising transport has a central place within the single market because of the economic importance of all branches of the transport industry and their vital role in moving goods between member states.

Completion of the single market in transport is scheduled for 1993, coinciding with the opening of the Channel Tunnel. It is particularly significant for the UK, where direct road and rail freight access into the European network will open up a major new opportunity for British manufacturers to compete with their EC rivals on more equal terms.

Airlines will have more freedom to fly the routes they want and set their own standard fares; moreover, there will be fewer restrictions on cheaper fares. It is likely that airlines' rights to fly between regional and local airports in different community countries will be extended, which will encourage new services, particularly from smaller airports (even now it can be cheaper to fly than go by boat or train). This greater freedom, however, will mean that the Community will have to action a substantial increase in air traffic control to ensure passenger safety.

6. Construction

The major impact will be from the public procurement directives, which will result in public construction projects being open to non-national suppliers.

The Commission recognises the need to accommodate good purchasing practice and the use of approved lists of suppliers, and this is particularly important in the very competitive construction industry where single projects can run into millions of ECUs. However, the European picture shows a far from level playing field (or building site) with public authorities in many areas refusing even to consider bids from outside their own country. Restrictive practices also include failure to advertise public contracts, discriminatory specifications including named national products and complex tendering procedures.

Besides widening the EC rules on purchasing, the Commission also proposes to implement an effective compliance procedure so that suppliers and contractors are able to pursue complaints about discrimination, and action can be taken against offending purchasers.

Despite the difficulties of harmonisation in this area the market is, nevertheless, extremely lucrative, and opportunities for co-operation within it are huge. Because of the size of many of the contracts involved, the formation of pan-European consortia for building contracts seems likely and it will be those companies best prepared to take advantage of the opportunities presented in this widening market which will benefit most.

7. Retailing

Harmonisation and standardisation, coupled with deregulation of distribution and payment systems, should all benefit the retail sector. For instance, until recently a guarantee for almost anything, be it a watch or a microcomputer, would have only been valid in the country of purchase. Now they must be valid all over the Community.

These changes could create opportunities in:

- Economies of scale.
- Acquisitions and mergers to gain distribution networks.
- Strategic relocation of warehouses and distribution points.
- Strengthening links with transport companies.

8. Financial services

The removal of barriers to the setting up and servicing of customers on a Community-wide basis will have three inter-relating effects:

- a surge in competitiveness;
- a follow-through to all businesses using the services: banks, insurance and the stock markets;
- a wider positive influence on the macro-economic policy of the Community.

At present, for instance, a simple life assurance policy underwritten by a British company in London can cost more than ten times more if offered by a Portuguese company. Restrictions on purchasing financial products outside the home country should, however, be removed by 1992. This will benefit British, Dutch, German and French financial institutions, which are already efficient and aggressive, but will adversely affect those in Portugal and Greece, which are not so strong.

4
STRATEGIES FOR COMPETING IN THE COMMUNITY

THE CURRENT SCENE

Given the opportunities which 1992 presents, and having considered the risk and the profit potential, how do companies begin a European marketing initiative?

The prospect may seem daunting, but closer analysis of the skills and knowledge required to commence activities will help in seeing opportunities; constant research in an ever-changing market place (and a vast market place at that) will bring things more into focus.

Every member state has recognised the importance of a truly open market. To ensure that the Single Market initiatives are understood and implemented, each Community state has undertaken projects to help not only their own business people but member nationals as well. Introductory marketing initiatives for 1992 are under way in most countries and in the other countries have at least passed the planning stage. An initial approach to the relevant country's agency should be the first port of call. Chambers of Commerce in each member state have also started their own initiatives, and again constructive help is available. However, before commencing, it is important to identify the target best suited to your products/services. Therefore knowledge of each country, its purchasing needs, consumer trends, etc, should be compared with your current and/or proposed service/product and analysed.

The Community covers a vast geographical area, spread over 2,253,000 square km, with a population in excess of 320 million. But the market, at least for consumer goods, is much more concentrated than these figures imply. Over three-fifths of the Community's population and its Gross National Product is found in a relatively small area, see Figure 2 on page 33. This 'Golden Triangle' generates some five to six times the amount of GNP than the areas bordering on the Mediterranean Sea. Thus, by closely identifying geographical regions of interests, the problem of scale can be reduced (to some extent) to target clearly the areas

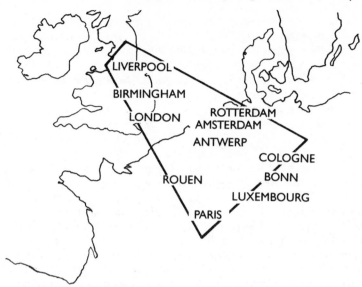

Figure 2 The 'Golden Triangle' of the EC
Source Butterworths, 1983

which can then form the basis for further market expansion.

The nature of political risk in the Community is in the attitude towards investment and industry. In Britain, for example, the UK Monopolies Commission needs to be consulted on major sector take-overs or mergers regarding the impact of change on UK consumers. In the context of the European market, the Commission also has to be consulted with regard to large investments, mergers or take-overs which could affect market positions and conduct of trade. (The decision-making bodies of the Community and the role they have in opportunities to undertake profitable business initiatives are discussed in Chapter 2.)

Large companies control over 50 per cent of the Community's total sales. Europe's 50 largest companies alone account for approximately 25 per cent of these sales. So, where does this leave smaller companies? Competitive advantages in timing and costs have always favoured the smaller company which can adapt quickly often leaving their larger competitor out in the cold. But more importantly, the concept of the Community helps.

The foundation of the Community is free trade, and so any business strategy which relies upon market-sharing, price fixing, exclusive purchase and exclusive or selective distribution agreements could fall foul of the Commission's regulations. However, the Commission has created a Business Co-operation

Network – the small and medium-sized business task force – to enable organisations to find contacts for collaboration. It has several channels for disseminating information: Euro-Info Bulletins, Target 1992, Euro-Information Centres and the Business Co-operation Network (B–C Net). In the UK, details of all these services can be obtained from your local DTI office, or from the DTI Hotline on 01-200 1992.

Euro-Info Bulletins and Target 1992 are newsletters obtainable regularly over the year. Euro-Information Centres, of which there are 39 in Europe (four in the UK), provide an interface between businessmen and the Commission, providing advice and answering questions on all aspects of the single European market. The B–C Net is a computerised network system that will eventually link small businesses with each other, with business consultants, banks, etc. The aim is to promote co-operation so that smaller businesses can compete with large companies on a more equal footing.

Strategic directions

Each state in which the company aims to operate will further complicate its marketing operations. A firm's well-thought-out corporate direction is critical to success. Arriving at any decision requires careful analysis and the following must be addressed:

- a corporate mission statement;
- set objectives;
- audit of research;
- option assessment: organic growth, acquisition, collaboration;
- evaluation of the realities of the company's position: what it is aiming for – a competitive edge, a market-dominant position, innovation?
- a plan for success.

For Community firms, it will not be simply a matter of opportunities; there will be disadvantages too. Their own domestic markets are sure to be affected as other Community firms expand beyond their own national borders. Neither will it be only European competitors; foreign companies (particularly the Japanese) are also being attracted by the harmonised market. The turbulence that can be created in almost all industries' traditional bases will require companies to create defensive strategies as well as expansive ones. Before setting a programme for Europe in order to take full advantage of 1992, five key points should be reviewed in building a secure base and protecting it from predatory companies:

1. Doing something is better than doing nothing – at the very least, undertake strategies which will increase the cost of entry into your own home market for foreign competitors.
2. Find a strong market position to defend, and do not retrench. Retrenching weakens the company's ability to maintain competitiveness.
3. Defend in-depth those areas of business critical to the company's success and survival. This can be achieved, for example, by denying to competitors segments and customers upon whom their entry to the market depends.
4. Attack competitors' weaknesses in terms of service, product range and marketing flexibility.
5. Protect the company's unity; weakness gives an advantage to competitors, unity gives confidence to the company and to customers alike.

THE IMPACT OF 1992 ON BUSINESSES IN THE COMMUNITY

Human resources

It will be enormously advantageous for businesses to have personnel who can not only negotiate successfully in a customer's own language, but who are also sensitive to cultural differences. These people need not necessarily be in senior management positions. In the UK for example, only about 4 per cent of management would claim proficiency in business French, but proficiency increases in key posts such as switchboard operators. Recruiting practices may change in response to the facility to recruit across borders. Organisations will need to review their training programmes in the light of the new opportunities presented in the Community.

In the ten years to 1986, the imbalance in the flow of professional and managerial persons in and out of the UK has grown to a two to one gain for the Community. In 1986, 17,700 managers and professionals went to Europe, whereas only 5,200 moved to the UK (figures quoted by IPS). Across Europe, there is an increased demand for highly skilled or service-industry workers, and a decline in opportunities for unskilled and manual workers.

Increasing attention is being paid to higher education as the source of entrants to the higher levels of the labour market. Continental degree courses are typically longer than in the UK, lasting four to six years. Vocational subjects such as engineering, business studies and law nearly always include substantial work placements. Recruitment reflects the need for vocationally-trained personnel, and very few untrained graduates are sought in such member states as the Netherlands, Spain, West Germany and the Republic of Ireland.

If continental graduate recruits are sought, the harmonisation of mobility of law and mutual recognition help, reaching these graduates will be more difficult in France and Germany, for instance, than in the UK. Recruitment is mainly carried out through personal links with academics, student work placements, direct advertising in newspapers and journals and the national employment services. Graduates are also more inclined to make speculative applications direct to companies. In general, continental graduates are older than UK graduates, and as such will require different training programmes and, usually, more senior positions.

Despite opinion to the contrary, the UK is doing something about language training for industry through the setting up of 20 'Language Export Centres' (LECs). These have been set up to help education and industry by attempting to resolve the language problems. One central telephone centre (on 01-934 0888) gives information as to the location of the LECs around the UK. These centres help to evaluate the strategic needs of organisations and then, with the assistance of the academics, provide linguistic training solutions. They are profit-making organisations.

Marketing and production

Strategic positioning of products and services may have to be reconsidered, not only in the light of the new opportunities, but also of the emerging threats. The 'golden' year of 1992 may be a useful public relations tool to all the company's audiences, but it is in the areas of research and development, distribution, purchasing, finance and accounting that the major impacts will occur.

FINANCE FROM THE COMMUNITY

The Community's budget includes a number of funds, such as the Social Fund and the Regional Development Fund, which promote Community objectives by financing suitable projects. Community financing can take the form of grants, low-interest loans, or participation in contracts funded by the Community. More financing opportunities are available from the European Investment Bank.

However, the operations of the funds and institutions are governed by complex and changing regulations and Community objectives. To help ascertain the acceptability of an applicant for finance, the Commission of the European Communities publishes a guide to grants and loans (a summary can be found on pages 37-41). Community financing has eight main purposes:

1. Employment and training.
2. Agriculture and fisheries.
3. Regional development.
4. Economic development.
5. Energy.
6. Coal and steel.
7. Developing countries.
8. Research and development.

In addition, funds are available for such projects as education, culture and transport.

Information on Community financing is available in the booklet entitled *Finance from Europe*, and can be obtained from 8 Storey's Gate, London SW1P 3AT (tel: 01-222 8122).

The European social fund

Non-repayable grants for certain employment and training, retraining, resettlement and job creation schemes are available from the European Social Fund. Applications for these grants are only eligible if the scheme assists a group of people or a type of operation within one of the Fund's 'areas of intervention'.

The European Agricultural Guidance and Guarantee Fund

The European Agricultural Guidance and Guarantee Fund (EAGGF, also known as FEDGA) has two sections. The Guarantee section provides support for agricultural products; the Guidance section supports a number of schemes to improve agriculture. The largest part of Guidance section funds is used to underpin national schemes to encourage structural development and to support agriculture in the less favoured areas.

The European Regional Development Fund

The European Regional Development Fund is intended to help eliminate the disparities in levels of development and wealth between different regions. The Fund goes hand-in-hand with national policies aimed at stimulating the economic development of underdeveloped regions by:

• the provision of financial incentives (grants, loans, tax

exemptions, etc) to businesses to encourage them to settle in these areas to create jobs;
• the development of infrastructures to enhance the development of these areas and attract investors.

The European Investment Bank

The European Investment Bank (EIB) is the Community's own bank, providing long-term finance for capital investments meeting Community priority economic policy objectives. Established by the Treaty of Rome, the EIB is both a Community institution, with the task of promoting European integration, and a bank, raising the bulk of its fund on capital markets, and lending the proceeds to projects meeting its eligibility criteria.

Finance for Energy

One of the Community's primary objectives is to ensure adequate supplies of energy for its future development. Financial support for projects conforming with this objective is available in a number of forms.

The European Coal and Steel Community

The European Coal and Steel Community treaty authorises the Commission to grant loans with an interest rate subsidy to certain investment projects in the coal and steel regions, and to certain low-cost housing schemes. Grants may also be awarded to help the resettlement or redeployment of coal and steel workers, and financial assistance is also available to help technical, social or medical research within the industry.

Aid for research and development

The Community research action programmes include three forms of research work:

• Directly-managed research carried out at the four establishments of the Community's Joint Research Centre.
• Contract research paid for (normally at a level of about 50 per cent) by the Commission and carried out by research organisations in member states.
• Co-ordination of research actions financed and carried out by research organisations in member states, and also frequently in European non-member countries. The Commission has a co-ordinating role, but makes no financial contribution except towards the cost of certain studies and the maintenance of the co-ordination machinery.

Miscellaneous funds

Education
There is no Community education fund. A limited number of pilot projects have been initiated in connection with the transition from school to work and the education of the children of migrant workers.

Transport
Transport infrastructure investment may qualify for assistance, provided the project is of Community interest. The projects most likely to qualify are those situated on major international axes and which are designed to facilitate the movement of goods and passengers within the Community.

Cultural programme
A limited number of pilot projects are initiated and funded by the Community in accordance with its cultural programme to improve vocational training and to stimulate employment in the cultural sector. There are also grants available for the conservation of the Community's architectural heritage.

Other funds
The Commission has very small funds which it can use at its discretion to grant subsidies to:

- Higher education institutions setting up a programme of value to European integration.
- Groups, movements, circles or activities of a European nature.
- Non-governmental organisations pursuing humanitarian aims and promoting human rights.

These funds are managed by the Secretariat-General of the Commission in Brussels.

HELP FROM THE COMMUNITY FOR SMALL-TO MIDDLE-SIZED BUSINESSES

Central to the development of an active and successful free market in Europe is the small- to middle-sized (SME) Business Task Force of the European Commission. The SME Task Force was established in 1986 to develop policies for small- and medium-sized businesses. The actual definition of what constitutes an SME is dependent upon the member state; in the UK it is VAT levels, in France the number of employees. European-wide addresses of the organisation's offices in each state are provided in the appendix to this chapter. It is expected that the actual number of offices should increase to 200 by the year 1992. The following extract, provided by one such unit, explains the function of the units:

'The European Community has embarked on an ambitious series of measures to help small and medium-sized companies. One such action aims to improve the flow of information to SMEs by setting up channels of communication and information on community activities. This will be achieved through the Centres for European Business Information which will not only supply firms with information and advice but also gather their suggestions on requests for specific services. the centres are set up within existing decentralised 'host' organisations in the member states, which have close contact with SMEs, in order to ensure that they can cater for firms' day-to-day needs.

'The Centres will be equipped with a computer-based system which will respond to requests for information on community activities. SMEs will be able to make enquiries on community information at the centres in person, or by post, telex, telefax or phone. For example:
(a)   The internal market – the legal, regulatory, social and technical aspects governing intra-community trade and the likely changes following completion of the internal market; opening up public supply contracts, etc.
(b)   EC's operational policies – community grants and financial instruments; research and demonstration programmes; sectoral measures; training schemes; regional policy measures and trade relations with non-member states.

'Where applicable, the centres will also provide help on completing application procedures and will co-operate with the EC's information offices on information campaigns directed at a wider public. The activities of the centres also include the organisation of, and participation in, national and international business events such as trade fairs, exhibitions and seminars. they will also stimulate co-operation between business nationally and internationally. The centres will prepare general information sheets and special packs in response to requests for assistance and advice; monitoring of local publications.

'The commission (SME Task Force) will provide the centres with basic community documentation regularly updated and access to EC databases, will be responsible for staff training and will meet part of the marginal costs of opening up the centres with a limited financial contribution in the first year. Within the SME Task Force there is a central structure, staffed with Information Officers, who are on hand to respond to enquiries from SMEs which the centres cannot deal with alone.'

In the UK, the Department of Trade and Industry (DTI) itself helps companies of all sizes to export directly to Europe. the DTI's regional offices are able to offer advice on the Export Initiative's support, which ranges from consultancy support to assistance in exhibiting overseas. The Exports to Europe branch in London is able to provide information on individual markets, and assist with enquiries about import duties, regulations and taxes.

Central to the development of the DTI's programme are the Regional Offices. These co-ordinate the needs of firms and help them to apply for consultancy funding of up to 15 days of a consultant's time. They also advise on the correct department for *ad hoc* desk-top market research sources. These addresses are listed on pages 42–43 of this chapter.

A STRATEGIC CHECKLIST FOR 1992

- Be aware of legislation and how it could adversely affect your business: be prepared to lobby if necessary. Do not restrict your review to Community countries; non-EC country negotiations can offer even more threats or opportunities.
- Identify what are the major likely changes for your business and conduct an internal 1992-readiness audit. *Do not* try to fool yourself as to your readiness.
- Identify and review the likely impact upon:

    (a) potential and existing customers;
    (b) suppliers;
    (c) existing competitors;
    (d) new entrants to your market.

- Evaluate the opportunties which arise to sell products or services in new markets by assessing the viability of entering new markets.
- Set up an overall review strategy for the challenges ahead, testing opportunities and threats against the company's aims and profit projections.

APPENDIX

If you need advice or information about any aspect of exporting to the EC from the UK, contact your regional DTI Office, or speak to an Exports to Europe Branch country desk:

Belgium, Luxembourg	01-215 5486
Denmark	01-215 5140
France	01-215 4762
Greece	01-215 4776
Ireland	01-215 4783
Italy	01-215 5103
Netherlands	01-215 4790
Portugal	01-215 5307
Spain	01-215 4260
West Germany	01-215 4796
General EC enquiries	01-215 5549

Or write to:

Exports to Europe Branch
Department of Trade and Industry
1–19 Victoria Street
London SW1H 0ET

UK Department of Trade and Industry's Export Initiative regional centres

Newcastle-upon-Tyne (North-East)	Stanegate House 2 Groat Market Newcastle-upon-Tyne NE1 1YN Tel: 091-232 4722 Telex: 53178
Manchester (North-West)	Sunley Tower Piccadilly Plaza Manchester M1 4BA Tel: 061-236 2171 Telex: 667104
Leeds (Yorkshire & Humberside)	Priestley House Park Row, Leeds LS1 5LD Tel: 0532 443171 Telex: 557925
Nottingham (East Midlands)	Severns House 20 Middle Pavement Nottingham NG1 7DW Tel: 0602 506181 Telex: 37143
Birmingham (West Midlands)	Ladywood House Stephenson Street Birmingham B2 4DT Tel: 021-631 6181 Telex: 337919

London (South-East)	Bridge Place 88/89 Eccleston Square London SW1V 1PT Tel: 01-215 7877 Telex: 297124
Bristol (South-West)	The Pithay Bristol BS1 2PE Tel: 0272 272666 Telex: 44214
Scottish Export Office	Industry Department for Scotland Alhambra House 45 Waterloo Street Glasgow G2 6AT Tel: 041-248 2855 Telex: 777883
Welsh Office Industry *Department*	New Crown Building Cathays Park Cardiff CF1 3NQ Tel: 0222 823185 Telex: 498228
Industrial Development Board *for Northern Ireland*	IDB House 64 Chichester Street Belfast BT1 4JX Tel: 0232 233233 Telex: 747025

Table 4.1 UK survey on Single-Market efforts

PHASE	ACTION	PHASE	ACTION
A. Initial Launch March/April/May 1988	1. SUPPORT LITERATURE 1.i) 'Why do you need to know more about the single market' – 129,000 mailed to medium and large organisations. 1.ii) Information pack of 25 fact sheets made available; Action Checklist 'Toward 1992'. 1.iii) Spearhead: online database. 1.iv) 1992 hotline: 01-200 1992 1.v) Videos produced by DTI – 'Europe Open For Business' and '1992 What's That?' 2. ADVERTISING 2.i) TV, press and poster campaign featuring leading business figures. 3. CONFERENCE AND SEMINARS 3.i) Lancaster House Conference opened by the Prime Minister (18 April 1988) followed by 20 regional conferences. 3.ii) Private Sector Seminars add an additional 2,300 as reported to DTI.	**C. 1989**	3. CONFERENCES AND SEMINARS 3.i) Regional Seminars sponsored by DTI finished in December. 4. NEWSLETTERS 4.i) First edition of the quarterly 'Single Market News' mailed in November. 1. SUPPORT LITERATURE 1.i) Third edition of 'The Facts' March 1989. Fourth edition of 'The Facts' September 1989. 1.ii) '1992 For You – An Action Guide for Smaller Firms' mailed to 214,000 firms plus an 200,000 insert campaign. 1.iv) 10 Standards Action Plan booklets produced (1 January 1989). 1.v) White Paper Checklist, giving information on the Commission's White Paper (April 1989). 1.vi) Series of guides produced or in the process of being produced. 2. ADVERTISING 2.i) 'Standard Action Plan' publication advertised in national and regional press. 2.ii) 'Action Guide for Smaller Firms' advertised in specialist press. 3. VIDEOS 3.i) 'Brussels Can You Hear Me', produced in March 1989. 3.ii) 'Signposts to 1992', produced in March 1989.
B. Extension of above May 1988–December 1988	1. SUPPORT LITERATURE 1.i) Second edition of 32 fact sheets 'The Single Market – The Facts' sent to 110,000 companies and individuals on DTI's mailing list. 1.ii) Second edition of 'Why You Need to Know More'. 2. ADVERTISING 2.i) Further phase of TV advertising (October–November) aimed at smaller firms.		

The total expenditure on the campaign to date is £13 million, of which £9 million has been spent on TV and press advertising. DTI ministers or officials have spoken at nearly 1,200 single market events to date.

5
THE EUROPEAN CONSUMER

POPULATION STRUCTURE

Much has been written about the unified market of 320 million potential consumers; larger than the United States, the Soviet Union or Japan. But it is not spread evenly across the whole geography of the Community. The UK, Italy, France, West Germany and Spain account for 83 per cent of the population. The density of the population measured in persons per square kilometre is greatest in the Netherlands, followed by Belgium, West Germany, the UK and Italy. The least densely populated country is the Republic of Ireland. The density obviously varies within member states and basically corresponds to industrial regions or administration centres such as Madrid, Lisbon and Naples. In Spain, there is a concentration in coastal areas, due to the influence of tourism since the late 1960s.

Demographic trends show a decline in the European birth rate since 1960, more pronounced and sustained than in the United States or the Soviet Union. The significance of this is brought more into perspective when the population replacement rate is reviewed against actual births. In only two countries, the Republic of Ireland and Spain, does the birth rate actually match or exceed the population replacement rate. West Germany's birth rate is 38 per cent below the replacement rate. The impact on economic, political and social policy for Europe is hard to evaluate; however, continued long-term decline will seriously reduce the market and change consumer purchasing trends. West Germany already has a decline in its total population.

The growth rate for the population of Europe is projected to increase (better health care and life expectancy) in the next 15 years, but only by 2 per cent. In the rest of the world, the projected figure is 36 per cent; in the United States and the Soviet Union 17 per cent; and in Japan 8 per cent.

CONSUMPTION AND PRICES

As might be expected, there is a wide variation in the Community in per capita GDP, with Luxembourg and Denmark up to 28 per cent higher than the Community's average, and Greece and Portugal 47 per cent below the average. Regional differences also occur, with GDP varying by up to 200 per cent between the north and south of Italy, and the north-west and south-west of Spain. These variations are reflected directly in purchasing power. The Danes, Germans and Luxembourgers have about twice the purchasing power per capita than, say, the Greeks or Portuguese. Compared with the other two major economic nations, the Community's average consumption per capita is much lower than the Americans and marginally higher than the Japanese.

The Community's rate of growth of consumption of goods fell after the 1973 oil crisis and only fairly recently, in 1982, did it begin to accelerate. In 1987 it matched the world's highest spending (and most wasteful) nation, the United States.

All Europeans obviously do not spend their money in the same way. Spending patterns vary from one country to another. For instance, in Denmark the amount spent on accommodation and heating, transport, communications and recreation is above average. By contrast, in Greece, one of the poorest of the Southern European countries, households spend about twice the average proportion of their income on food, drink and tobacco. The growth areas across Europe are transport, communications and recreation, particularly in Belgium, France, the Netherlands and the UK. Consumption of foodstuffs and clothing is only increasing in Greece.

As spending patterns shift, so too does the relative cost of goods and services. And it is because of this economic shift that the Community is beginning to build a consumer policy. The impetus for such a move is the opening up of the Community's markets to member states for products from those countries. With such a policy, consumer protection also has to be taken into consideration, both in terms of its positive influence, ensuring confidence and awareness in the consumer to make his purchasing decision and in preventing non-tariff barriers being erected in the name of consumer protection.

CONSUMER PROTECTION

In some respects, consumer protection has been one of the last policy areas to be addressed by the Community. No mention is made of it in the Treaty of Rome; in fact, it was not until 1972 in Paris that heads of state of governments asked the Community institutions to prepare a programme aimed at strengthening and co-ordinating measures on consumer protection.

Within a few months, the Directorate-General for the Environment, Consumer Protection and Nuclear Safety was set up. In September 1973 the Consumers' Consultative Committee (CCC) was set up, representing the European Bureau of Consumers' Unions (EBCU), the Committee of Family Organisations in the European Communities (Coface), the European Community of Consumer Co-operatives (Eurocoop) and the European Trades Union Confederation (ETUC). Each of these four organisations elects six representatives, and there are nine independent experts.

In 1975, it presented the preliminary programme of the European Economic Community for consumer protection and information policy. Within the programme were contained five basic consumer rights:

- the right to health, protection and safety;
- the right to protection of economic interests;
- the right to redress;
- the right to information and education;
- the right to representation.

A second programme, adopted in 1981, reaffirmed these five rights, and put special emphasis on value for money as a matter of concern for consumers.

The CCC worked hard in the uphill struggle of harmonisation of standards, but with little success. However, the current approach is that the freedom of trade will not have to wait for the completion of technical work on standards. Once the essential health and safety criteria are provided for by Community-wide legislation, the standards of each state will be recognised by the others, and products complying with standards may be traded freely.

This new approach (work is still being undertaken by the European standardisation bodies, CED and Cenelec (the European Committee for Standardisation and the European Electrotechnical Standardisation Committee) in preparing common standards) was caused by a landmark judgement given by the Court of Justice concerning the *Cassis de Dijon* case. This judgement meant that the free movement of goods did not have to await the establishment of common standards.

Measures have been adopted in three main areas of health and safety:

1. Foodstuffs. These are lists of permitted substances and parity standards have been established for foodstuff additives such

as colourings, antioxidants and preservatives. Regulations have been introduced to govern the production of such foods as cocoa, tinned milk and chocolate. Directives have been introduced on the labelling of foodstuffs, specifying ingredients, quantity and date by which they should be consumed. Drugs and chemicals used for the rapid growth of animals for human consumption, and pesticides, have been banned or restricted.

2. Dangerous substances. Directives control the classification, marketing and labelling of toxic substances. The Community Directive 76/769, issued in 1976, provides for the banning of substances.
3. Pharmaceuticals. The testing, patenting, labelling and marketing of pharmaceutical products are all controlled by EC directives.

In 1984, the Council of Ministers established a system for a rapid exchange of information on dangerous products and substances. This was particularly effective after the Chernobyl disaster.

Although all of the directives are important, and the reader is referred directly to the Commission to ensure the compliance of his products, the most important concern of this chapter is economic safety: the ability of the consumer to determine whether the purchase of certain goods and services can satisfy his needs. The risk shared between supplier and consumer – have I made the right product? Is this product exactly what I want? – has swung in favour of the producer. In the first consumer programme, the Commission recognised this. It states:

'The consumer . . . has become merely a unit in a mass market, the target of advertising campaigns and of pressure by strongly organised production and distribution groups. Mergers, cartels and certain self-imposed restrictions on competitiveness have also created imbalances to the detriment of consumers.' (*Source* OJC 92, 1975, page 3)

Three areas are now considered: advertising, contract law with direct selling and credit.

ADVERTISING

Advertising, harmony and access are critical to the development of a free market. Restrictions on the advertising of individual products can directly affect their exporting prospects. Although individual country practices are to remain, it has been agreed that legislation is needed to regulate advertising to remove and avoid barriers to trade as well as to prevent deception of consumers. A directive adopted in 1984 prohibits misleading advertising, defining this as:

'any advertising which in any way, including its presentation, deceives or is likely to deceive the persons to whom it is advertised or whom it reaches and which, by reason of its deceptive nature, is likely to affect their economic behaviour or which, for these reasons, injures or is likely to injure a competitor.' (*Source* Directive 84/450, OJC 250)

This means that consumers or organisations may, if they believe they were misled, bring a complaint in law or to a competent administrative authority. In the UK, an amendment to law gives full power to this directive. Even more, the burden of proof is not with the consumer, but with the advertiser to prove the truth of his statements. The courts are also empowered to prevent or halt the publication of advertising.

Developments in satellite and cable television have brought a wider problem; that of pan-European broadcasts which, sent from one member state into another, avoids the stricter regulations in the latter state. In such a situation, the only way to regulate is by international consensus. A proposal was tabled by the European Commission in June 1986 to cover production, distribution and copyright. For broadcast advertising, five broad principles are stated:

1. Advertising must not offend against prevailing standards of decency and good taste.
2. It must contain no racial or sexual discrimination.
3. It must not be offensive to religious or political beliefs.
4. It must not exploit fear without good reason.
5. It must not encourage behaviour prejudicial to health and safety.

Tobacco and alcoholic drinks would be hit, as would advertising addressed to children and young people.

CONTRACT LAW AND DIRECT SELLING

'Purchasers of goods and services should be protected against the abuse of power by the seller, in particular against one-sided contracts, the unfair exclusion of essential rights of contracts, harsh conditions of credit, demands for payment for unsolicited goods and against high pressure selling methods.' (*Source* OJC 1975)

That is how the 1975 initial programme set out the principle of protecting consumer interests. However, as yet very little has been done to redress the balance at present so strongly in the favour of those large institutions which trade just the right side of the member state's laws.

The Community has taken some action only in regard to direct, doorstep selling. Adopted in 1985 (Directive 85/577, OJC) it deals with the conduct of agents calling uninvited to a consumer's home. The directive provides for a 'cooling-off' period of seven days following the signature of certain contracts, during which period the signatory may cancel the agreement. This right does not apply to contracts of insurance, securities, or mail order sales, or to contracts with a lower value than 60 ECUs.

CREDIT

Access to credit in other member states is to be a very important part of the consumer's post-1992 freedom. A directive adopted in 1986 (Directive 87/102, OJC) provides basic protection by requiring credit agreements to be made in writing and either the cost of the credit or the annual percentage rate of charge to be made clear. Under preparation is the standardisation of the way in which credit charges are expressed. All forms of credit are covered, including personal loans, credit card accounts and premanent credit allowed by suppliers and instalment sales.

SOCIAL CHANGE AND ITS IMPACT ON EUROPEAN MARKETING

This topic is built around the work carried out by Elizabeth H. Nelson in association with RISC (Research into Social Change). She has been able to identify social changes which are truly pan-European.

Although the starting point and speed of change in attitudes of 'Mr Average' from each country differs, consistency in trends appear. Using the RISC European Socio-Cultural map, the position of each country can be plotted. The position of the country on the map depends upon where the bulk of its population falls. For example, more people in France, Italy and Spain live in the northern half of each country, while UK, West Germany and the Netherlands have more people living in the southern half. The UK has changed its position in the past five years, moving more rapidly towards the centre than Germany.

Social change is mapped across two axes. The horizontal axis positions information-gathering from close family links and working environments: 'roots'; and a less restricted, more flexible, wider social contact environment based on personal interests developed: 'networking'. People high on this trend have a wider group of social contacts which are regularly changing. Because they seek out groups of people for information, rather than relying on a small number of references, they are usually better informed.

The impact on the promotion of products is important. It could create a move away from major branded campaigns to direct marketing. It is proposed that fewer people are likely to identify with slogans which suggest 'largest' or 'most modern' products, but rather will buy ones which they perceive to possess certain qualities which will meet a particular need. Large multinationals are becoming aware of a need to provide homogenous images where a heterogenous personality would be more appropriate. This is particularly true of American Express's European advertising.

The vertical axis is similar in many ways to Maslow's 'hierarchy of needs'. In the southern section of the map, fixed survival needs still predominate, whilst the northern section is more self-expressive and less nationalistic, with a greater acceptance of and capacity to manage change. For instance, in the late 1940s and 1950s, Europe had a strong commitment to the work ethic. Today with technology allowing more free time, whilst providing increased national prosperity, there is a general decline in the work ethic. This decline has been matched by an increase in the expectation of personal pleasure, greater interest in consumerism and a growing concern for controlling the influence of technology, particularly its impact on the environment. The 'Green' issues are an increasingly influential factor in all European attitudes. They are strongest amongst the young and better educated.

Other trends identified are moves towards:

1. *Polysensuality.* The desire for, say, consumers to smell fresh bread or coffee as well as to consume it.
2. *Open citizenship.* The loss of a degree of sovereignty, with consumers seeing themselves more as European than French, German or British. The understanding of the economic Europeanisation is growing in the UK, but more slowly than in the rest of Europe: Italy and France are well ahead.
3. *Achievement and risk-taking.* There seems to be a clear trend that people in more demanding and interesting jobs work longer and longer hours, blurring the work/leisure time distinction. A higher level of risk is accepted to gain success. Fashion and 'smart buys' are important to those showing this trend.

4. *Strategic opportunism.* There is a move away from complex, detailed research of business and personal decisions, towards a more aggressive, 'go for it' mentality.
5. *Exploring mental frontiers.* This is the growing feeling that we do not know enough about how we think and feel. This leads to an increasing reliance on emotion and intuition in making decisions.

The map depends upon the acceptance of Community social values. The evidence that some such element exists is in the global marketing successes of multinational brands such as Coca Cola, Walkman, Marlboro and McDonald's. However, understanding social cultural trends helps to fine-tune campaigns in order to achieve better results. Nielsen quotes pasta as an example:

'In every European country outside Italy, people who eat pasta frequently tend to be at the forefront of social trends, but people in Italy who eat a lot of pasta are backward on the trends. Therefore, a successful marketing policy for pasta in Italy would be very different from that in other countries.'

There is a convergence of trends amongst those who are at the forefront of change. The similarity of attitude in students, businessmen and professionals across Europe is significantly higher than people in those same countries who live in part of the south-west corner of the RISC map. The marketeer must take advantage of the trends, and apply his knowledge of the direction in which societies are moving. Merely satisfying customer needs is passive. According to Pepsi Cola's John Scully, 'The purpose of marketing now is to anticipate, persuade and influence'.

6
THE UNSPOKEN WORD

In conducting business with fellow Europeans there can be the inevitable problem of language. This is likely to remain the case, certainly for the language-shy British and certain other EC member states, for at least the rest of this century.

Learning European languages has to become an essential part of trading in the future. However, that is only part of the solution. As well as the standard written and spoken word, there is another factor that should not be overlooked – body language, or as the social psychologists call it, non-verbal communication (NVC).

Complications result when people verbally say one thing, but communicate a completely different thing with body language. Which one do you believe? Between people of the same nationality this can be difficult, but in mixed cultures it can be totally confusing. For instance, if an Italian puts his thumb and forefinger on his lips, what does this mean? What it actually signifies is sewing the lips together and he is telling you to be quiet. You might have guessed this, because it is a fairly close universal gesture, ie putting the forefinger on the lip. But what if you were wrong? It could turn out to be very embarrassing.

If there is a conflict between the verbal message and the physical, then generally the social psychologists and body-language experts say that we should trust the physical communication as being the accurate one. However, across nations and cultures it becomes harder to distinguish and separate these differences and understand the nuances – but it is important to be aware where variations may lie.

Therefore, it is not just what people say that is important, but also how they say it, and this is likely to involve body-language in one way or another. It is crucial to be able to interpret and read the true meaning of gestures or expressions.

Fortunately, within Europe, while there are a number of particular variations or national characteristics, there are, thankfully, many common gestures or expressions which are common ground for all. The variations are most extreme in Northern Europe compared with the Mediterranean area.

Facial expressions

The face can convey a multitude of diverse messages, but it is possible to make a generalised summary of these, at least as far as they are likely to affect business transactions. For practical purposes, it is possible to concentrate on the six key emotions of happiness, sadness, anger, disgust, surprise and fear. Across Europe, there is a reasonable closeness of expressions for most of these, though it does become harder to distinguish the difference between fear and surprise.

For Germans, there is some divergence from the more open expressions and there is a moderation or balance between the norms of the expression and the meaning conveyed. This divergence occurs on the following basis.

Table 6.1   Expressions and their meanings

Expression	Meaning
smiling	dominant
raised brows	happy
lowered brows	dominant

For most Europeans, these are fairly closely correlated, but Germans may be somewhat at variance.

The ability of Europeans to decode each others' expressions seems to be good – certainly better than trying to read non-Europeans, for example, the Japanese. In tests carried out, English and Italians scored highest at reading their own national intentions and also each other's.

For the gaze, or what is more normally referred to as eye contact, again European behaviour tends to be fairly commonly held. Europeans seem to be capable of accommodating our mannerisms to the degree which is acceptable and not intimidating to the other partner in the conversation. However, Southern Europeans seem to be more intense here and one notable exception seems to be the Greeks, who are much keener on a continuous eye contact and likely to be offended if your eyes start to wander from theirs. They prefer direct eye contact and because of this it would be difficult to hold a meaningful conversation with a Greek whilst walking side-by-side down the street, or if you were wearing sun-glasses.

Gestures

With regard to gestures, it is reassuring to discover that many of our conventional gestures are universal throughout Europe. These include pointing, shrugging shoulders, patting people on the back, head nodding, thumbs down, clapping, waving and beckoning. However, while the head nod for 'yes' is common, there is some disparity with the head-shake for 'no'. While Northern Europeans recognise the head-shake, in Greece this is replaced by the head-toss.

Generally, there is less use of gestures in Northern Europe and greater use in Southern Europe, with France possibly taking the middle ground.

Another gesture you may come across is the pursed hand. Seldom seen in the UK, this has a number of different meanings throughout Europe; in France, it stands for 'fear', in Greece 'good' and in Italy it signifies a query.

Italian gestures you should look out for are the open hand put in front of the face with fingers and thumb spread. If you see this gesture, it could mean that the business negotiations are not going too well (the sign actually represents 'gaol')! If the Italian starts to make a sign with thumb and fingers put up to the eye forming a monocle, this is a rather scornful way of telling you to watch out – a form of disbelief at what you are saying.

For emotional display, the facial gestures are fortunately fairly common to all, and you will be on reasonably safe ground interpreting that shaking the fist indicates anger; yawning, boredom; touching the face, shame; showing the palm of the hand and lowering the hand, submission.

The North and South divide

Under the heading of 'spatial behaviour', for practical purposes it is helpful to split Europe into the North and South divide. For this, the contact cultures separated from the non-contact cultures. Broadly speaking, the former are represented by the South, and the latter by the North. For the contact races, there is a stronger tendency to stand closer to people, have more face-to-face contact, touch more often and speak in a louder voice. For Northern Europeans, it could be necessary to adjust your behaviour to cope with this, whilst not duplicating their actions at least being able not to be put off by it.

Looking in more detail at how close people stand to each other, studies in the past have indicated that the Southern Europeans will stand about two feet from each other, but the distance will more likely be over three feet between Northerners. A number of generalisations can be drawn from this which would seem to indicate that the Northern Europeans are less physical than the southerners.

Again, the same study seems to support this view by considering the interaction as witnessed by touch and the use of the voice. For Southerners, the voice is much louder and there is a greater preponderance of touching, reflecting warmer and more intimate behaviour.

The problems here would seem to focus around trying to seek the right balance with the business relationship; if you stand too far away you may find that your partners see you as distant and unfriendly. On the other hand, if you invade their personal territory you might embarrass them and be seen as intrusive and overfamiliar. As a general rule, it is a good idea to spend a little time trying to observe these differences closely. It is best to take your cue from your host/buyer, but stay alert and be willing to adapt your behaviour as different cultural circumstances demand.

The British are not great 'touchers' and studies have shown that these characteristics are also shared with the Germans and Dutch. However, the Southern Europeans and French are prone to be more expressive. In one study a comparison of touching found that the number of touches per hour made by couples in cafés was 100 for Paris, and zero in London.

SOME EUROPEAN CONTRASTS

The OK sign

In Britain, to signal 'OK, fine', the hand is raised and a circle is made with the thumb and forefinger. In France, that gesture alone means 'zero' or 'worthless'. In Greece, it is an obscene insult to either male or female.

The nose tap

Tapping the side of the nose in Britain is a meaning of secrecy or conspiracy, but in central Italy it signifies 'take care, there is danger, they are crafty'.

Eye touch

This is where the forefinger touches the face just below the eye and pulls the skin downwards, opening the eye wider. In France, it means 'you can't fool me, I see what you are up to'. In Italy, it means 'keep your eyes peeled, pay attention, he's a crook'.

Chin flick

The back of the fingers swept upwards and forwards against the underside of the chin in France means 'get lost, you are annoying me', but in Greece it is not an insult, just a negative 'I don't want any' or 'I cannot'.

Nodding/shaking the head

The nodding and shaking of the head to indicate yes and no are fairly standard, except in Greece where the rhythmical movement of the head from side to side can mean 'yes' rather than 'maybe yes, maybe no'. And for 'no' the Greeks will tilt their heads sharply back and return it less sharply to the neutral posture.

Hand waving

In Britain, the lateral wave dominates, while in France the vertical wave is more usual and in Italy the hidden palm wave, similar to beckoning, replaces both.

PART 2
A COUNTRY BY
COUNTRY GUIDE

7
BELGIUM

INTRODUCTION

Belgium is a country of two nations, or, more accurately, of one nation speaking two different languages: the North speak Dutch and the South speak French (except in the western Liege province, where there are German, French and protected Dutch-German speaking communities). An understanding of the differences is useful, as they can have a major impact on businesses which span the two areas. Nowhere else in Europe does one nation have two quite distinct ethnic and linguistic communities: the Germanic Dutch-speaking Flemish in the North and the Latin, French-speaking Walloons in the South. To complicate matters, Brussels is a largely French-speaking island situated 20 miles into Flemish territory.

For the Briton, the language division can be a positive advantage, as it creates a common communication channel: English. Its usefulness is based on its neutral status and can be used in all regions of Belgium.

Central to the European concept with Brussels (the home of the EC Commission and a key community city), being the EC host capital, historically Belgium has generally looked towards its neighbours for trade. It was one of the founder members of the Community. The Belgian people do not regard their linguistic homelands in a separate way as, for instance, do the Scottish Nationalists in the UK or the Basques in Spain, they are proud of their monarchy and enjoy the sense of unity and national identity which it bestows.

Today, Belgium is mainly an industrialised nation. A close relationship is still maintained with Luxembourg, whose currency is tied to the Belgian franc. Class and education snobbery in Belgium is not usual; however, whatever beneficial transaction is done for one of the main language groups will have to be matched for the others.

MAKING THE APPOINTMENT

The meeting should be arranged initially by letter, which should be written in English unless you are sure of the language in use: Antwerpen Dutch, Mons French, etc. English is recommended if writing to a company in Brussels, but at all times bear in mind the delicacy of the situation.

A letter should be well written (particularly if it is in business French) and you should offer to provide an interpreter at a subsequent meeting. Badly-written letters are likely to be rejected immediately, although any attempt to communicate in Dutch rather than French is more appreciated in the South. A letter can be followed up within two weeks of sending. When following up the letter, however, do note that the Belgian postal service is not the fastest in Europe!

The secretarial role varies from region to region; generally, in the North, the secretary is more likely to hold the executive's diary and to act on his behalf. Be careful how you address the secretary as informality is only acceptable after an appropriate length of time.

THE MEETING

If the letter is written in English, there is no insistence on interpretation, but as mentioned before, to provide a French or Dutch speaker for the meeting would be appreciated. When attending a meeting, the European custom of hand-shaking will apply across both cultures. Small talk is reserved for generalities, and getting down to business will occur quite quickly. Coffee or tea will usually be served at the meeting.

Formality is still very much the norm on the first meetings, with the initial meeting conducted on surname terms. Only after the relationship has continued for several meetings is the use of first names likely. It is also important to be on time: if you are late, then your appointment is likely not to be honoured or will at least be restricted which is not a good start.

Family life is important to Belgians, and they set aside time for it. They will also visit their extended families regularly, as often as once a week.

Belgians see themselves as more efficient, more reliable and producing higher quality goods than most other countries. Belgians also believe themselves to be more hardworking and less friendly, at least at the beginning of a relationship. They are more cautious than, say, the Dutch.

ENTERTAINING

Business meals

Breakfast meetings are unusual in Belgium. Breakfast is taken at home; although early morning meetings are not uncommon, but it would not involve having a meal.

The likelihood of a lunch invitation has little to do with your rapport and more to do with the focus of the business proposition and the point it has reached. Lunch will normally take between one and two hours, starting at noon. The person extending the invitation normally pays the bill. Eating out is customary in Belgian, so ask your host for the names of appropriate restaurants if you are extending the invitation.

Dinner invitations are usually longer and less frequent than lunch. If the invitation is for dinner at the person's home then it certainly shows a progression in the relationship since Belgian people do tend to separate home from business life.

If you are invited home, you should bring flowers with you; do not bring any form of drink. When you meet the lady of the house, shake hands; cheek kissing only occurs once greater familiarity is achieved.

Belgians are famed for their hospitality, so be forewarned. If a Belgian decides to take you out on the town, it will be a long and expensive business. It is best to decline until the negotiations are concluded, as it is very difficult to match practised Belgians at socialising particularly if a meeting is scheduled for the following day!

In all dealings with Belgians, be prepared for the best of everything; if you are entertained, particularly at home, you will be utterly spoiled.

Subjects for social discussion

When making small talk, bear in mind that the Belgians set great store by their homes, the same applies to the town or city in which they live. Remarks about the town or city if made in positive statements are helpful, as are comments on family life. Whatever else you discuss, never mention the language division as this is a very delicate topic.

Business hospitality

Other than in the cultural centres of Belgium, opportunities for business hospitality are limited. However, the Belgians are unlikely to commit company marketing budgets to corporate hospitality. One-to-one meetings, perhaps an invitation to an important sports event, are more likely to be offered, based on your host's personal interests.

Gifts

Gifts should be restricted to the functional, logoed business object. Extravagant gifts will be rejected.

Dress

It is very important to dress well and stylishly. Men should wear dark suits, shirts and ties – the tie should remain on in all circumstances. For women, trousers are usually unacceptable, as are short skirts; stockings or tights are always worn, even in summer.

WOMEN IN BUSINESS

In Belgium, the role of women is changing rapidly. They are not, however, employed in the most senior jobs in the country. Belgium has the highest female unemployment percentage in Europe, but its general rate is on par with the rest of the Community.

WORKING HOURS AND PUBLIC HOLIDAYS

The usual working day starts at 8.00 or 8.30 am, lunch is taken between 12.00 and 1.00 pm, and the day finishes around 6.00 pm. The normal holiday entitlement is four weeks, split into two two-week holidays. Summer holidays fall in with school holidays, which are taken during July and August. Unlike the UK, Christmas, New Year and Easter are restricted to the basic holidays plus a day or two.

1st January	(New Year's Day)
1st May	(Labour Day)
21st July	(National Day)
15th August	(Assumption)
1st November	(All Saint's Day)
11th November	(Armistice Day)
25th December	(Christmas Day)

In addition there are three movable days, including Easter.

LETTER-WRITING

For letter-writing, see the appropriate sections on the UK, the Netherlands and France, pages 88, 142 and 178. If in doubt about which language to use you should opt to write in English.

MARKETING

The marketing spend in Belgium remained fairly constant in line with media inflation until recently, when a small increase occurred. The country's bilingual nature has resulted in a split in level of infrastructure which supports Belgian-built agencies. Belgium, therefore, has a large number of agencies of American origin. Another reason for the increase is because of its culture and communication channels Belgium provides an ideal testing ground for European campaigns. The major changes in marketing spends are an increase in below-the-line activity and a greater investment in direct marketing.

Socio-economically, the country is split into four groups:

Table 7.1   Socio-economic grading in Belgium

	%
A	3
B	16
C_1	46
C_2	15
Other	20

Source   CIM

The media, in Belgian francs, is spread in the following way:

Table 7.2   Media spend in Belgium

	%
Newspapers	24
Freesheets	9
Consumer magazines	33
Television	16
Radio	2
Cinema	1
Outdoor, transport	15

Source   AAS/CACP

The spend rankings by key categories are:

Table 7.3   Spend categories in Belgium

(1)   Automotive
(2)   Department stores
(3)   Finance
(4)   Clothing, shoes
(5)   Alcohol, wines, beer
(6)   Cosmetics, hair-care

Source   AAS

Media

There are no special advertising taxes. VAT is levied at 19 per cent. Advertising is not allowed on national state-owned TV and radio channels, except 'non-commercial' generic information-style advertisements and public service announcements. Alcohol advertising is not allowed on TV or radio. Certain restrictions exist on outdoor advertising. Tobacco advertising is not allowed on TV or radio and in the cinema only basic information is allowed, such as the pack and the price; it must also carry a health warning. Restrictions on advertising tobacco outdoors include a restriction on the size of the poster/billboard to no more than 16m². Press advertisements for tobacco are restricted to no more than half a page per brand in newspapers and one page in magazines. There are severe restrictions on most pharmaceutical advertising. For further information contact: Jury d'Ethique Publicitaire, Rue des Colonies 54, PO Box 13, 1000 Brussels (Tel: +32 2 219 06 62).

CONSUMER PREFERENCES/DIFFERENCES

Household spend

The Belgians take great pride in their homes. As such it is not surprising to find that they spend a considerable amount of money on purchases for their home.

Belgium ranks third in consumer spend on home furnishings and is at the top of the spend category for the whole range of household electrical appliances. The consumer spend on the latter could be considered essential to their way of life as opposed to a consumer preference.

Because of the work pattern in Belgium (and the same applies for Denmark), basic household appliances, which ease the workload at home, can be found in 90 per cent of all households. These appliances include washing machines, fridges and vacuum cleaners. For example, food processors sales in Belgium are the highest in Europe.

The Belgians love of all things beautiful in their home by no means stops at the convenience or essential level. In the EC spend on items such as tableware and cutlery Belgium again tops the list. Another high area of consumer spend is in the level of board games. Belgian ranks close to the top of the sales in the market penetration of home computers. Although interestingly, ownership of video machines is one of the lowest in the EC.

The population in Belgium is about 10 million and, although smaller in comparison to the population of France or Germany, the consumer demand represents a good target market for manufacturers of home-related appliances.

The statistical breakdown of household spend on domestic goods and services is as follows:

Table 7.4   Belgian household spend

Items	%
Furniture (including carpets and other floor coverings)	29
White goods	15
Furnishings	10
Tableware and utensils	17*
Domestic and other household services	29

Source   Eurostat/Mintel
*Note** the highest spend in EC.

Financial awareness

Most major banks have a presence in Belgium, and bank services are well used, for example, 71 per cent of Belgiums have a bank account compared to the UK figure where only 45 per cent of the populace have a bank account (although this figure has shown a marked increase over the last 10 years). Credit cards are not considered essential, however, with only 5 per cent of the population holding a card. Building societies are not used as much as banks with only 17 per cent of the population holding accounts.

Food spend

The introduction of hypermarkets is well accepted with 75 per cent of people shopping there.

In meat consumption, the Belgians' preference is for pork and they spend very little on mutton, lamb or goat. Fish on the other hand, is regularly consumed.

The Belgians are the third largest consumer of meat *per capita* in the Community. To wash this down Belgians drink more mineral water than anywhere else in Europe and drink more beer *per capita* than the English!

General consumer spend

Foreign designed clothes rank high on Belgian preferences in clothing. They clearly prefer to buy clothes from foreign designers rather than their own industry. But compared to their European partners, the Belgians do not spend a great deal on clothes; indeed, they spend more on beer than they do on clothes!

When selecting a car or consumer durables Belgians will buy products made in their country rather than purchase foreign-made items.

Political trends

Although the green issues put forward by the Ecologist Party showed the Belgians have a keen interest in their environment, the Socialist Party just 'pipped' the Christian Democrats gaining eight seats as opposed to seven.

Voter awareness of issues is high with a 93 per cent turnout of voters. Belgium has 24 Euro seats.

ESTABLISHING A BUSINESS

Prior authorisation is only required for certain types of business; for example, transport, insurance and banking.

Most foreigners who do business in Belgium set up a limited company, either private or public. Both types of company are governed by the same 'company laws'; accordingly, the major differences being in the size of capital and the nature of shares. No special consents are needed, except in certain closely defined activities relating to specific products. Statutory documents must be deposited with the Belgian equivalent of Britain's Companies House system. Each year 5 per cent of each companys' profit must be put into a legal reserve until the reserve equals 10 per cent of the issued capital. This reserve may not be distributed, but there is no other limitation on the repatriation of profits.

Foreign companies can operate in Belgium through a subsidiary, incorporated under Belgian law, or through a Belgian branch of a company. The following types of company may be used although a corporation, *Naamloze Vennotschap (NV)* or *Société Anonyme (SA)*, is most common.

- corporation (SA–NV);
- private limited company (SPRL–BVBA);
- general partnership (SNC–VOF);
- limited partnership (SCS–VEG);
- partnership limited by shares (SCA–VGA);
- societé cooperative (S Coop–Coop V).

The minimum legal capital for a SPRL–BVBA is BF 750,000, and for a SA–NV, BF 1,250,000. Both are governed by the same legal requirements, but only a SA–NV can be listed on the Stock Exchange. Shares in a SPRL–BVBA are represented by 'parts sociales'.

A subsidiary set up as a Belgian company is required to comply with Belgian company law, whether or not the shareholders are foreign nationals or companies. Company directors may be foreign nationals. There is no legal requirement that a Belgian national should own part of the share capital.

Every corporation must file its articles of incorporation, the names of its directors and statutory auditors, and its annual financial statements at the appropriate Register of Commerce.

Foreign companies may set up branches in Belgium. Branches are governed by the same regulations as Belgian companies as regards management and operations in Belgium; they must appoint local representatives and register certain documents.

Foreign companies wishing their Belgian branch to engage in trade or manufacture are required to file a certified copy of the parent company's articles of incorporation together with any amendments with the Trade Register of Commerce. A statement by the parent company's board authorising the establishment of the branch and the delegation of powers to the branch management, and the name and address of its official representative in Belgium, should also be filed.

The branch must also register with the Register of Commerce where it is located, obtain a registration number and keep appropriate legal and accounting records.

Management structure

A SPRL–BVBA is managed by one or more directors, who do not have to be holders of *'parts sociales'* or company shares. They are elected by the shareholders. Once elected they are allowed to run the company in whichever way they see fit, inside or outside the objects of the company's articles of incorporation. They have to prepare an annual inventory, accounts and management report for the shareholders.

In a SA–NV, the company is managed by at least three directors, appointed at a general meeting. They have the ability to delegate the daily management of the company, but are liable to third parties for transgression.

Since 1986, all companies meeting the following criteria have to appoint a statutory auditor:

- annual turnover of BF 145,000,000;
- balance sheet totals of BF 70,000,000;
- annual average of 50 persons employed.

In a SA–NV company or SPRL–BVBA, if there are more than 100 employees, a workers council of equal numbers of employer and employee representatives must be set up. A meeting must be convened at least once a month to review working conditions and the progress of the company. It is seen as a co-operative association.

SINGLE-MARKET EFFORTS

Government

The State Secretariat for Europe 1992 was created in May 1988 to disseminate information on the Single Market, and has a budget of 700,000 Belgian francs for 1988/89. A 1992 hotline, 'Europhone', opened in June 1988, and TV commercials aimed at the general public began on 3 October 1988.

Business

Employer's federations, trade associations and Chambers of Commerce are all concentrating on small and medium-sized enterprises.

Surveys

Of those questioned, 35 per cent in the latest survey had no opinion at all on the implications of 1992 for Belgium. Of the remainder, 53 per cent were optimistic about the prospects. A regional split was evident, with 50 per cent in Flanders expecting to benefit from the Single Market, but only 40 per cent in Wallonia expecting to do so.

USEFUL ADDRESSES

Sources of information and help

Belgo–Luxembourg Chamber of Commerce in Great Britain Inc
36 Piccadilly
London W1
Tel: 01-434 1815
Tlx: 8953411 BELCOM G

British Chamber of Commerce for Belgium and Luxembourg
30 Rue Joseph II
B-1040 Brussels
Tel: (+32) 02 2190 788
Tlx: 64580 BRICOM B

Research sources

A.C. Nielsen Company (Belgium) SA
Avenue des Arts 56
B-1040 Brussels
Tel: (+32) 02 5112296
Tlx: 21794

Aspemar SA, (full market research service)
Avenue des Arts 2
Boite 16
B-1040 Brussels
Tel: (+32) 02 2191100
Tlx: 65409 ASMAR B

Addresses for advertisers

Jury d'Ethique Publicitaire
Rue des Colonies 54, (details of advertising restrictions)
PO Box 13
1000 Brussels
Tel: (+32) 02 2190662

Association des Grandes Enterprises de Distribution, (major retailers representative body)
Rue de la Science 3
B-1040 Brussels
Tel: (+32) 02 5373060

Chambers of Commerce

Brussels   Rue de Trevs 112
1004 Brussels
Tel: (+32) 02 512 3030

Antwerp   Markgravestraat 12
Antwerp
Tel: (+32) 03 232 2219

Principal Euro Info Centres

Euro Info Centre
Avenue Sergent Vrithoff 2
B-5000 Namur
Tel: (+32) 81 73 52 09

Euro Info Centre
Markgravestraat 12
B-2000 Antwerpen
Tel: (+32) 03 233 7658

8
DENMARK

INTRODUCTION

Denmark, despite its reputation as the land of fairy tales and make-believe villages, is in reality a sophisticated nation whose economic centre has shifted away from agriculture to service and light industries. It has a flexible manufacturing base the entrepreneurial spirit of which is thriving.

Denmark is a liberal-minded, tolerant, compact nation with a low crime rate, a deep sense of social welfare and strong co-operative links with immediate neighbours. Danes have a great sense of humour and are much more interested in the good life than in power and politics. They also react with stubborn resistance to outside pressure.

A strong entrepreneurial spirit is evident within the business structure, and there is a constant spin-off from larger firms into smaller companies. More than half of all industrial jobs are in companies with under 200 staff.

MAKING THE APPOINTMENT

Beginning a business relationship with a Danish company requires a formal approach. It is best to write the initial letter in English and ensure that it states the purpose and the goals of the proposed meeting. The Danish attitude to language is similar to the Dutch in that they recognise the smallness of their population (and land mass) in relation to the rest of Europe and consequently know that they must adapt to speaking other languages. Even so, it would be appreciated by your Danish counterparts to offer to provide an interpreter, particularly if you are dealing with one of the smaller, family-owned companies, the head of which may not be used to negotiating in a foreign language.

The secretarial role as a well-defined one and, as in most Northern European countries, the secretary plays a significant part in the organised business life of your Danish counterpart. You may assume that she is an extension of the individual to whom you wish to speak.

THE MEETING

The Danes' one obsession is with punctuality, so do make sure you arrive on time for appointments, whether business or social. If you know you will be more than a few minutes late, ring. Once at the meeting, small talk is limited. Be prepared for hardheaded, direct discussions and have all the facts at your fingertips.

The Danish language reflects, as do French and German, the closeness or formality of a relationship. When discussion is in English, formality is always best, but will be relaxed very quickly, given the potential for a good rapport, particularly if your business contact is fairly young.

Danes do not go in for lengthy haggling, and they expect that your proposition will be thoroughly worked out before you present it to them. If they are going to do business with you, it is because they have identified you as an expert in your market, and they will expect the proposition to reflect that. The Danes are likely to walk away from a poorly-put business proposition, even when they know (from past experience or previous introduction) that you have a worthwhile product, so it is important to be thorough and precise.

Their high standard of living should make the Danes a consumer market. They are aware of this, and expect imported products to be of the highest quality in order to compete with their home-produced goods.

The 'moralistic', rather dull, image of the Danes may be an accurate prejudice so far as business meetings are concerned, but the subsequent relationship is usually very far from being dull, indeed it will probably prove to be quite the opposite. The Danes' reputation for admirable organisation should not be confused with restrictiveness and limitations.

ENTERTAINING

Business meals

The Danish breakfast, being a substantial meal (cheese, meats, eggs, cake, bread and gallons of coffee), is an opportunity for business meetings. The Danes begin work between 8.00 and 8.30 am and finish between 4.00 and 5.00 pm. Only half an hour is normally taken for lunch, the British and Spanish lunch culture is certainly not apparent in Denmark. Business lunches do occur, but more likely (perhaps because of the size of breakfast) is the offer of a business dinner.

Dinner may be taken at your host's home or at a restaurant. It is unlikely that being invited home will be of any significance to your business transaction. Your business counterpart's partner is likely to attend, even if you dine at a restaurant.

Should you be invited home, then flowers are the most appropriate gift for the hostess. The bouquet should be produced by a florist, and presented wrapped, to the hostess. It is also important to telephone and thank her the following day. A gift of whisky or brandy (*not wine*) is considered appropriate for the host.

Subjects for social discussion

It is irritating to the Danes to be confused with other Scandinavian countries as it is for the Scots to be referred to as English or for that matter for the French-speaking Belgians to be mistaken for French nationals. An understanding of Danish geography, industrial infrastructure, history and major businesses will create a good impression: for example, in literature, Hans Christian Andersen and Karen Blixen; in science, Professor Bohr; in business, the major international companies of Bang and Olufsen, Lego and Danfoss. If you can also differentiate between Sweden, Norway and Finland, your acceptability will be enhanced.

Avoid discussions about the German occupation during the Second World War; discussions on the family, the house and non-controversial subjects are suitable topics. An appreciation of the high quality of Danish design and of their food would also be well received.

Business hospitality

Business hospitality is not formalised in the same manner as it is in the UK. The type of hospitality offered will be moulded to the interpersonal relationship. No lavish corporate entertainment industry exsits.

Gifts

These are usually restricted to company logoed pens, ashtrays, etc. It is important only to give such items if they are deemed to be stylish. The low standard of design incorporated in such items produced by many companies worldwide will do nothing to enhance your relationship or business presentation.

Dress

Business dress is less formal than in other countries in the EC, for example, in the UK and Germany. Blazers, suits and sweatshirts are all acceptable modes of dress for the Danish businessman. Do not, however, assume such informality yourself, at least initially. A conservatively-styled suit, in a dark colour, with an appropriate tie and black shoes would be expected; save your jeans for sightseeing!

WOMEN IN BUSINESS

The high cost of living in Denmark has perhaps played an important role in introducing women in to business life than previously admitted. It is quite common for both spouses to work away from home, and it then goes as a rule that the work-load associated with cooking, childcare and cleaning is shared. In this environment, male dominance in business has been more quickly eroded than in most Northern European country members of the Community; of the number of applications for the Danish police force, 40 per cent of those received are from women. The Danes also have female tank crews.

WORKING HOURS AND PUBLIC HOLIDAYS

The Danes, as already mentioned, begin work fairly early in the day and finish after about eight hours. They take five weeks' holiday a year, of which three will usually be taken during July, as school holidays start in June and finish at the beginning of August. Christmas and Easter holidays are shorter than in the UK.

The major public holidays are:

1st January	(New Year's Day)
1st May	(Labour Day, afternoon)
5th June	(Constitution Day, afternoon)
25th 26th December	(Christmas Day)

There are six other movable public holidays, including Easter.

LETTER-WRITING

The envelope

English	Danish
Mr	Hr (forename[a], surname)
Mrs	Fru (forename, surname), or
	Fr (forename, surname)
Miss	Frk (forename, surname), or
	Fr (forename, surname)

Salutation

Letter written in:	
Danish	English
Kære Hr (surname)	Dear Mr (surname), or Dear Hr (surname)
Kære Fr (surname)	Dear Mrs (surname), or Dear Fr (surname)
Kære Fr (surname)	Dear Miss (surname), or Dear Fr (surname)
Not used	Dear Sir, Madam

Closing		
Individual	med venlig hilsen	Yours sincerely
Company	med venlig hilsen	Yours faithfully

Note
ᵃ The full forenames should always be written. It is usual practice to write initially to the department of the firm or organisation, not to an individual

MARKETING

Commercial TV, cable TV and radio are the growth areas in advertising. Advertising as a whole in Denmark is affected to a greater extent by economic cycles than it is in most other European countries. 1988 was a poor year and 1989 is not expected to be much better. However, the new media opportunities, combined with increased competition and squeezed margins, will eventually result in strong, high-profile agencies which will get stronger. The growth in the industry, if it occurs, is likely to be in the public and semi-public sectors: Post, Giro, Telecom and railways.

The Danish consumer is not standarised into groups by socio-economic classifications, so for marketing purposes one or more criteria such as income, housing, age and geographic location can be used.

The advertising krona is split as shown in Table 8.1.

Television advertising became available for the first time on 1 October 1988, and the figures are not yet available.

The spend rankings by key categories are shown in Table 8.2.

Table 8.1   Advertising spend in Denmark

	%
Newspapers	32
(Copenhagen	15)
Magazines	8
Freesheets	7
Cinema	1
Outdoor	2
Direct response	50

Source   Danske Reklambureauers Brancheforening (DRB)

Table 8.2   Danish consumer spend

(1)	Cars
(2)	Department stores
(3)	Financial
(4)	EDP equipment
(5)	Magazines
(6)	Beer
(7)	Non-alcoholic beverages

Source   Gallup Markedsanalyse

Media

There is no special advertising tax. VAT is charged at 22 per cent. There are press restrictions on advertisements for alcoholic beverages, pharmaceutical products, tobacco and lottery promotions. New instructions have been issued by the Minister of Culture and Communications concerning the content of advertisements on the new television channel. Among other things, the advertising of alcoholic beverages containing more than 2.25 per cent alcohol is banned. Also banned are tobacco products, medicines and political, religious and economic interest groups such as business associations and unions. A special set of rules concerning advertising to children and the use of children as models has been issued. For further information contact: Consumer Ombudsman, Bredgaede 31, Copenhagen 1260 (Tel: (+45) 1 138711).

CONSUMER PREFERENCES/DIFFERENCES

Household spend

The Danes can be regarded as the perfectionists of the EC. They insist upon stylish, well-made products; they are suspicious of products from other nations.

The Danes spend a considerable amount of money on home furnishings and electrical appliances. Perhaps because both partners work, these 'preferences' can almost be classed as essentials.

Like the Germans, the Danes prefer clear, bright definitions of colour in any article they buy.

Financial awareness

Denmark is an expensive country to live in compared to its member states in the EC.

The bank system in Denmark is a sophisticated one, on par with the rest of Northern Europe.

Financial products, as known in the UK, are gradually becoming known, although there is some consumer resistance.

Food spend

All pork products are favourites. Fish is second on the Danes list of preferences.

Consumption of other staple food products is average as is beer, wine and spirits.

General consumer spend

Denmark's population is circa six million, but despite this, the consumer spend is strong. The criteria when selecting goods has to be quality above all else.

Political trends

In Denmark, as in the UK, the loser in the Euro election was the Conservative Party. Out of a total of 16 Euro seats the Conservative's total was reduced from four to two.

Voter apathy is not quite as pronounced as in the UK, with Denmark second from the bottom of the turnout table with 46 per cent.

ESTABLISHING A BUSINESS

Danish branches of foreign companies and all Danish companies must be registered in the Register of Companies (*Aktieselskabs-Registeret*). Other enterprises that carry on a trade or business must be registered in the Register of Commerce (*Handels-registeret*). However, sole traders are not obliged to register. Licences to trade are not required.

The two main types of company are private (*Anpartsselskab*, or ApS) and public (*Aktieselskab*, or A/S). Both are limited liability companies.

New businesses with an obligation to deduct tax from workers' or employees' pay must also register with the Central Tax Assessment Office (*Statsskattedirektoratet*) and businesses which are subject to value added tax (VAT) must also register with the VAT authorities. Social insurance registration is automatic following the notification to the Central Tax Assessment Office. There is no requirement to belong to any Chamber of Commerce or trade association.

The construction drawings for the erection or alteration of any building must be approved by the technical department of the municipality concerned.

No special rules apply to borrowing money within Denmark by Danish enterprises owned by non-residents.

Management structure

Every public limited company must have a Board of Directors (*bestyrelse*), consisting of at least three members. Substitutes or alternatives for individual directors may be appointed.

The Board of Directors must appoint a manager or board of managers (*direktion*). The managers are responsible for the day-to-day operations of the company, the Board of Directors being responsible for supervising the managers, laying down general policy making decisions on unusual transactions. All the managers, and at least half of the directors, must reside in Denmark (whatever their nationality) or be EC nationals resident in other EC member states. (The Ministry of Industry can, however, grant exemptions from this rule in certain circumstances.)

Members of the board of managers may serve on the Board of Directors but must always constitute a minority on that board. Corporate bodies cannot be appointed as either directors or managers.

If the articles of association so provide, the shareholders may elect a board of representatives (*repraesentatskab*) whose function is to supervise the directors and managers, but in practice such a board is rarely appointed.

In companies with an average of at least 35 employees (including hourly-paid workers) over the last three years, the employees are entitled, if they so wish, to elect to the board at least two further directors or half the number of directors elected by the shareholders (rounded up, if necessary, to the nearest whole figure), whichever is greater. In any company in which the employees exercise their entitlement, therefore, the minimum size of the Board of Directors is five. In addition, any group of companies (as defined by Companies Law) that has had an average of at least 35 employees over the last three years must, according to special rules, allow its employees to elect representatives to the Board of Directors of the parent company, if they so desire.

Works councils (*samarbejdsudvalg*), made up of equal numbers of representatives of management and labour, may be established in enterprises with at least 30 employees, if either the employer or more than 50 per cent of the employees so require. Rules as to works councils are usually laid down in collective agreements; although only members of employers' associations that are parties to those agreements are obliged to follow these rules, in practice all employers concerned do so. Works councils do not have any management powers or rights of veto over directors' or managers' decisions; they are principally used to communicate with and inform the employees. Individual councils' rules can stipulate the particular circumstances in which employees must be informed.

SINGLE-MARKET EFFORTS

Government

A campaign was launched at the beginning of October 1988, with the release of information packs and advice brochures. There is a budget allocation of krona 3.25 million. Information packs are obtainable by ringing 01-992 1992.

Business

The Danish Industry Council launched an advertising campaign on the Single Market, aimed at the general public, on 21 November 1988. The campaign ran for two months with a break for Christmas. They have also produced a series of short leaflets with general Single-Market information.

Surveys

No government surveys have been commissioned as yet, although one private survey among accountancy firms on the preparation for a Single Market showed 50 per cent confirming that they had a 1992 strategic plan, and 31 per cent preparing such a plan. However, 70 per cent said they felt that from the competitive point of view, Danish industry was not yet ready for a Single Market.

USEFUL ADDRESSES

Sources of information and help

British Import Union
Borsbygningen
DK-1217 Copenhagen K
Tel: (+45) 1 136349

Research sources

Gallup Markedanalyse (part of Gallup organisation)
Gamnel Vartov Vej 6
DK-2900 Hellerup
Copenhagen
Tel: (+45) 1 298800
Tlx: 15180 GALLUP DK

Vilstrup Research (qualitative and quantitative
   research)
Godthabsvej 187
DK-2720 Copenhagen Vanlose
Tel: (+45) 1 866677
Tlx: 22988

Addresses for advertisers

Consumer Ombudsman (details of advertising
   legislation)
Bredgage 31
Copenhagen 1260
Tel: (+45) 1 138711

Danske Reklamebureaurers (Association of
   Danish Advertising Agencies)
Branchforening
Snaregade 12
1205 Copenhagen K
Tel: (+45) 1 134444

Chambers of Commerce

Copenhagen   Børsen (Stock Exchange)
                        1217 Copenhagen K
                        Tel: (+45) 1 155320

Principal Euro Info Centres

EF-Radgivnigskontoret for Fyn
Noorregade 51
DK-5000
Denmark
Tel: (+45) 9 146030

EF-Radgivnigskontoret
Haselgaardsvaenget 18–20
DK–8210 Arlins
Denmark
Tel: (+45) 625 0318

9
FRANCE

INTRODUCTION

French chauvinism is perhaps the overwhelming attribute of French business life. Some have likened it to arrogance based upon a long-past era when the French and the use of the French language were the centre of the diplomatic world. Today, you are at a distinct disadvantage in negotiations if one of your team does not speak good business French, for that is the language in which business will be conducted if the meeting is in France.

The French lifestyle is also changing. The Paris-based executive is much more of a Eurocrat, taking shorter lunchtimes and focusing more on the business goal. Staying late at the office is almost a status symbol, such status symbols being very important to the French. French business still has a strong affinity to the old money business families and great respect is also shown to the new breed of financiers who control, through holding companies, large sections of the business scene. A privatisation programme had begun, but was stopped due to the world stock market crash of 1987. The Paris scene is particularly rigid and formal, but on the Mediterranean coast and in the Midi people tend to be more accessible and more vague about timekeeping.

Snobbery in education is as significant in France as it is in the UK: being part of the Grands Corps de l'Etat. These are graduates of the Grands Ecoles (usually Ecole Polytechnique or Ecole Nationale d'Administration). This backs up the marked class division that still exists, based more on background than on wealth. Only 13 per cent of university and college students come from working-class families.

In all business transactions with the French, it is best to remain formal and conservative. Do not be surprised by initial negative reactions to new ideas, and do not expect any snap decisions. A Frenchman is complimented by your respect for his nation and his culture (a good appreciation of his food and wine is also well received). He is hard in negotiations, expecting everything from courtesy to concession from his partner. These requirements are not necessarily matched by himself: a French negotiator who will speak in English is very much in need of the deal!

MAKING THE APPOINTMENT

The role of a secretary, for many French executives, is little more than that of a typist. Many senior executives still open their own post and keep their diaries, so what may seem like unco-operative behaviour from a secretary may simply be lack of knowledge. It is not unknown for letters to go unacknowledged for weeks because the boss is out of the office. However, a secretary can be an important influence in securing appointments, and it is worth developing a rapport, if you can.

French business is conducted very formally, and an initial interview is best requested in writing, and before the suggested date. The letter must conform to the best in business French. A poorly-constructed letter will lose impact or be totally disregarded. Address the letter to the head of the firm. Seek an initial meeting with the President/Directeur General, and send your most senior person to the meeting. Older people, in particular, like being called by their titles and if someone has several it is best to address him by the one he feels is most important, even if it is historic to his current job. Some managers do seem to think it increases their prestige to wait until very close to the appointment date before replying. Be on time and well prepared for the meeting; they will expect you to be even if they are not themselves.

Initial contacts and more complex discussions usually take place in the firm's offices with experts and advisors present. Always shake hands when entering a meeting with all those present and those joining the meeting, and do the same on leaving. Do not expect refreshment during the meeting; this is not the custom. It is hard to over-stress the pride the French have in their achievements, whether it be sporting or economic. An awareness, and even appreciation, will be well received. Small talk, however, is limited in business meetings, which should be conducted in French. To assume that English (or any other language) will be spoken, even if you have had initial contact outside France in a business setting or social contacts within France and spoken English, will be to assume incorrectly as this will not be the case at the meeting. If you, or a member of your team, is not fluent then the meeting might just as well be cancelled. It is not unusual for the French businessman or official in such cirumstances to stand and leave the meeting.

THE MEETING

Although younger people are more informal, the French still set great store by formal courtesies, titles and the right dress. It is safer to address your business partner as *monsieur* or *madame*, and to let the French set the pace.

Because of the legalistic nature of the French, every deal will tend to be drawn up in meticulous detail. Once the document is signed, however, it may be treated with a great deal of ambivalence. They will hold you to every letter of an agreement, while trying to find ways around it to suit themselves. The French have two kinds of rules: the written and the ones for actual use. Subtle tactics and good presentations are very important. Be well prepared, with good, solid, rational arguments and show commitment and enthusiasm. The French style of negotiations can include the switch of tactics to turn any negotiator on to the defensive even when responding to a French proposal. Once the deal is done, it will be hard work keeping to the terms. If you in any way do not match your commitment then you are likely to be sued. If they do not, look very carefully at the wording of the deal. It is always important to take contact notes of any business meeting and ensure acceptance of any decisions in writing and in detail.

Even if you have managed to develop a friendly rapport with your business partner, do not be surprised by the formality of his business letters. In France, anything put in writing is a serious business!

ENTERTAINING

Business meals

The breakfast meeting is fast establishing its place in the businessman's diary. Breakfast may be held in an hotel, a firm's executive dining room, or even a café. The meal will be more substantial than is usual for a normal French breakfast.

France is renowned for its cuisine and its lavish restaurant lunches. Business lunches can take up to three hours and will usually be very relaxed functions. Business in unlikely (naturally) to be discussed until the coffee stage, although to raise it earlier may be acceptable. Whoever issues the invitation should pay the bill, and it is quite acceptable for you to issue the invitation. However, remember that the French have a high regard for good food, so it might be appropriate to ask your guest to select the venue. It is likely to be expensive.

There is a movement away from the extended lunch, which is only likely to occur on occasions of success and celebration. In day-to-day relations, a quick brasserie lunch is common.

There is no special significance attached to being invited to dinner (unless it is to your host's home), which is fairly common in the provinces. Sometimes the host will bring his wife, but don't suggest it unless you have already met. If you should be invited to someone's home, you should follow the accepted niceties of not talking business until the coffee and brandy arrive, and not smoking before the cheese. As gifts, choose flowers or good chocolates for the hostess and malt whisky or cognac for the host – never wine!

The French are quite an hospitable race once you have passed their French admiration tests. Business entertaining may be cultural or sporting and should not be turned down. If you are invited away for the weekend, do make every effort to attend.

To conclude, the French will hold you strictly to the deal while it suits them, and breach it when it does not. Examine contracts very carefully as they can, and often do, lead to acrimonious relationships. Enter relationships on a long-term basis, for the short-term business deals will be difficult to achieve but, if you are successful in the longer term, the association could lead to a very good and profitable relationship.

Subjects for social discussion

Until fairly recently, it would have been quite unacceptable to talk about the cost of living or the size of your salary (although you might have been surprised at the openness of discussion about extra-marital relationships). French society has, however, become much more consumer-oriented of late, and people are more often judged by their success in business than they were in the past. French introversion should be respected, however, complimentary comments on their culture and wine would be well received.

Business hospitality

Grand hospitality at sponsored events does not occur as it does in the UK. Invitations may be given to the opera, a concert or to society horse race meetings.

Gifts

Gifts from the company such as a pen or diary with the company logo are acceptable. Very expensive gifts may cause offence.

Dress

Style is important to the French, thus dress should be smart, erring on the side of conservatism. Men will almost always wear a suit and tie, and women smart, chic, classic clothes. Even in hot weather, you would not be expected to shed your jacket and tie if your French host retains his. Dark suits are appropriate in Paris throughout the year, with lighter suits being acceptable in the summer.

WOMEN IN BUSINESS

France has accepted the role of female executives as well as any European country. In commerce, women hold senior, middle and junior management positions. In industry, however, some prejudice still exists. Women are expected to retain their femininity, even as successful business people in 'a man's world'.

WORKING HOURS AND PUBLIC HOLIDAYS

The Parisians, in particular, work long hours, starting in their offices as early as 8.30 am and finishing at 8.00 in the evening. The French executive feels he deserves to take his weekend and holidays seriously: they should not be disturbed. Holidays are long – four to five weeks in summer and two weeks in winter. Because of these holidays, business usually stops from about mid-July to early September.

The main public holidays are:

1st January	(New Year's Day)
1st May	(Labour Day)
8th May	(Victory Day)
14th July	(Bastille Day)
15th August	(Assumption)
1st November	(All Saints' Day)
11th November	(Armistice Day)
25th December	(Christmas Day)

There are, in addition, three movable days, including Easter.

LETTER-WRITING

The envelope

French	English
Monsieur (first forename[a], surname)	Mr
Madame (first forename, surname)	
Mademoiselle (first forename, surname)	Miss

Salutation

	Letter written in:	
French		English
Monsieur[b] or if known Cher Monsieur		Dear Mr (surname)
		Dear Monsieur (surname)
Madame, or if known Chère Madame		Dear Mrs (surname)
		Dear Madame (surname)
Mademoiselle		Dear Miss (surname)
		Dear Mademoiselle (surname)
Monsieur, Madame		Dear Sir, Dear Madam
Closing		
Individual	Je vous prie d'agréer, (monsieur) l'expression de mes sentiments distingués	Yours sincerely
Company	Je vous prie d'agréer, messieurs, l'expression de mes/nos sentiments distingués	Yours faithfully

Notes

[a] Initials are only used if the first name is not known. Except at senior level, it is normal to write to the particular department concerned, and not to the individual.

[b] If the letter is written in French, the surname is always omitted in the salutation.

MARKETING

The economic environment of France is stabilising, while expenditure is rising. Total expenditure on advertising is rising at over twice that of household expenditure. Media advertising grew by 14 per cent in 1987, and all areas of marketing services are currently experiencing growth. Television advertising has increased at the cost of radio and cinema. France has a success-ful pay TV channel – Canal Plus – with over two million subscribers. The press, however, remains the main medium with over 55 per cent of the total budget.

The classification of consumers is based on household income, and is:

Table 9.1   Consumer spend on household income in France

			%
A	=	FF 15,850 per month or above	15
B	=	FF 9,680–FF 15,850 per month	30
C	=	FF 5,390–FF 9,680 per month	40
D	=	less than FF 5,390 per month	15

Source   SECODIP, Chambourcy

The split in advertising in the media is approximately as follows:

Table 9.2   Media spend in France

	%
Newspapers	24
Magazines	26
TV	21
Radio	10
Outdoor	17
Cinema	2

Source   IREP, Paris

The spend rankings by key categories are:

Table 9.3   Key spend categories in France

(1) Household appliances
(2) Food
(3) Retail trade
(4) Leisure, entertainment
(5) Toiletries, beauty products
(6) Beverages
(7) Clothing
(8) Culture, tourism

Source   SECODIP, Chambourcy

Media

All media are subject to VAT at 18.6 per cent. Pharmaceutical advertisements must be approved by the health authorities and are subject to a tax of FF 1,000 when placed by the authority for examination. Tobacco advertisements are allowed in the press only, but the annual total amount of money allowed to be spent by tobacco products in the press is restricted according to a special formula based on previous investments. Copy in a tobacco advertisement can only name the product and show its packaging, composition, trade-mark and name and address of the manufacturer and/or distributor. Outdoor posters related to smoking are prohibited. Also, companies will be required to devote at least half their advertising budget to low-tar products. Targeting of children is strictly forbidden. Advertisements for alcoholic beverages are restricted in all media and forbidden on TV except for drinks up to and including 1° strength alcohol. All alcoholic advertising in sports grounds and all places where educational events take place is forbidden. Even where advertising is allowed in the press, a warning has to be included urging moderation in drinking. Also forbidden on TV are advertisements for the press, cinema, shows and retailers. For more information on advertising contact: Association des Agences Conseils en Publicité (AACP), 40 Boulevard Malesherbes, 75008 Paris (Tel: (+33) 1 4742 1342).

CONSUMER PREFERENCES/DIFFERENCES

Household spend

Although not as houseproud as the Belgians, the French level of spending on household products is high when compared to other countries in the EC. Domestic and household appliances (electrical sector) show that sales are 2 per cent higher than the Belgian spend.

As far as environmental issues are concerned, the French, Germans, Dutch and Italians are more aware and show the greatest concern and this is reflected in their purchase preferences of products and foods.

The French bask in the knowledge that they are considered to be the most chic and elegant of nations. Mute, pastel shades are common choices of colour not only in soft furnishings but in the colour schemes of other products, from household appliances to clothes.

The breakdown of household spending on domestic goods and services is as follows.

Table 9.4　French household spend

Items	%
Furniture (including carpets and other floor coverings)	31
White goods	16
Furnishings	7
Table utensils	15
Domestic and other household services	31

Source　Eurostate/Mintel

Financial awareness

Over the last few years the French have become more sophisticated in financial matters; fast disappearing is the image of suit-
cases of gold stashed under the bed. Another example of this
increased financial sophistication is that the French now have
the highest level of purchase of unit trusts in the EC. Overall on
investment, however, they consider savings to be at the bottom
of their preference list.

Next to the Germans the French have the highest percentage
of personal bank accounts. Major international banks have a
presence in most provincial cities as well as Paris. Moreover,
the French have the highest percentage of penetration of credit
cards.

Food spend

The French method of shopping has changed quite radically
over the last decade, showing a 24 per cent increase in the use of
hypermarkets and supermarkets.

The French cuisine is known and enjoyed worldwide and the
French are duly proud of this. Surprisingly however, fresh fruit
consumption is lower than that found in Germany and the UK.
Meat consumption figures show that France heads the league
consumer table in canned meat and canned fish consumption,
the spend on the former, *per capita*, is valued at approximately
US$ 26 million. The French are at the top of the spend list in the
EC for meat consumption, having equal taste for pork, beef and
veal but overall spend more on fish than meat. Purchase of
canned fruit and vegetables are also very high.

Per capita, France has the highest consumption of butter in
the EC with 28.2 per cent. As would be expected cheese consumption is high, in fact the second highest in the EC.

Not unexpectedly as it is one of the major wine producers,

France has a very strong home market and the wine consumption percentage is 34.7 per cent.

General consumer spend

When given the opportunity to increase their spending, the first preference for the French is a day out or a holiday while the lowest desire is to save and investment. Credit is therefore an important and attractive consideration for the French when selecting which item/items to buy.

Belgium is the market leader in total purchasing volume of clothing, but the French are not far behind.

In the percentage spend on passenger cars, France is fourth behind West Germany, Italy and England.

Political trends

The notable gains in the Euro election in France were made by the Green Party, who hold nine out of a total of 81 Euro seats. The 'green' issue is seen to be important.

France recorded 49 per cent voter turnout but is still below the average EC total of 59 per cent.

ESTABLISHING A BUSINESS

A foreign-owned enterprise in France has the same legal status as a French-owned one, and the government does not insist on French participation.

The two most important forms of company are the *Société Anonyme* (SA) and the *Société á Responsabilité Limitée* (SARL). The main difference between the two is that equity in the SARL is closely held, while in SA is it not normally restricted to the founders of the company.

Every new enterprise must be registered in the Companies and Commercial Register, giving information on its constitution and details concerning its offices. The lease on offices and sometimes the residence permit of the General Manager must also be submitted in support of the application.

New businesses must also report to the local direct and value added tax authorities and the social security office. A signed copy of the constitutional documents must be submitted to the registration duty authorities for payment of the duty.

A zone certificate, showing the company's proposed activity is permitted, must be obtained from the Ministry of the Environment in the department concerned. New buildings require a building permit from the mayor of the commune, plus, in Paris, the Ministry of the Environment. Local building controls are complex, and numerous anti-pollution measures are in force.

Management structure

A corporation may choose between two different systems of management:

1. a single administrative board *(conseil d'administration)* by a president who usually acts both as chairman of the board and chief executive of the corporation; or

2. a two-tier system comprising an executive committee *(directorie)* and an independent supervisory board *(conseil de surveillance)* which oversees the activities of the executive committee.

Very broadly, the functions of the chief executive in the single-tier system correspond with those of the executive committee in the two-tier system, and those of the administrative board in the two-tier system. A corporation may change from one form of management to the other by decision of the shareholders. The single-tier system is still the more widely used.

In the single-tier system, the administration board consists of three to twelve directors *(administrateurs)* who are elected by the shareholders. Larger boards are permitted in limited circumstances. The first directors of a private corporation may be named in the articles, in which case each serves for a maximum of three years. In all other cases, a director is elected for a maximum of six years.

Board members, including the president, are personally liable for any mismanagement of the corporation. Contracts between board members and their corporations must be specifically approved.

The supervisory board in the alternative two-tier system consists of three to twelve members whose appointments and procedures are broadly similar to those of administrative board members under the single-tier system.

The executive committee consists of two to five members who are appointed by the supervisory board for fixed terms of four years. They may be removed from office only by the shareholders in general meeting on the advice of the supervisory board. Members of the committee do not have to be French nationals or shareholders, but must be individuals. The committee is responsible for the day-to-day management of the corporation and is given the widest powers of representation. It must submit a quarterly report on the corporation's activities to the supervisory board, and is responsible for producing year-end financial statements.

In the two-tier structure, only the president of the executive committee, if from a non-EC member state, needs to hold a commercial card.

Employees of at least two years' standing may be appointed as members of an administrative board, although not more than one-third of the members at any one time could have employment contracts with the corporation. The two years' standing requirement does not apply if the corporation is formed after 1 January 1988. Employees may not be members of a supervisory board but may be appointed to an executive committee.

Any corporation with 50 or more employees must establish a works committee (*comité d'enterprise*). This body may send two representatives to attend meetings of the administrative or supervisory boards, but not to meetings of the executive committee. These representatives have no voting rights at such meetings.

SINGLE-MARKET EFFORTS

Government

A campaign relaunch is due in 1989. The impact and value of the previous campaign, which was a high-profile, television advertising campaign, is being evaluated. Much of the theme and execution was also evident in the UK Department of Trade and Industry's awareness advertising.

Business

A major conference was organised by the French Patronat on 13 December 1988, which was attended by 4,000 employers. The accent was on encouraging small and medium-sized enterprises to plan for 1992. The Patronat will follow this with seminars on specific issues, and is continuing to disseminate general information on the Single Market.

Surveys

A recent survey showed a drop in business confidence that France will do well from the Single Market. Of those questioned 12 per cent (against 22 per cent in 1987) thought that France would be one of the two countries benefiting most from 1992, and 63 per cent (against 71 per cent in 1987) thought that the Single Market would be an opportunity rather than a handicap to French industry. The general level of awareness was shown to be not as high as in the UK.

USEFUL ADDRESSES

Sources of information and help
British Consulates General in France
11 Square Duttileul
59800 Lille
Tel: (+33) 20 578790
Tel: 120169

Research sources
A. C. Nielsen
44 Boulevard de Grenelle
75737 Paris
Tel: (+33) 1 4578 5120
Tlx: 270868

Addresses for advertisers
Association des Agences Conseils en Publicité (French Association of Advertising Agencies)
40 Boulevard Malesherbes
75008 Paris
Tel: (+33) 1 4742 1342

Association Nationale du Marketing-Recherche et Strategie-Action (major marketing association)
30 rue d'Astorg
75008 Paris

Chambers of Commerce
Bordeaux   12 Place de la Bourse
33076 Bordeaux
Tel: (+33) 56 909128

Lyon   Palais du Commerce
Lyon
Tel: (+33) 7 842 2575

Marseilles   Palais de la Bourse
13222 Marseilles
Cedex 1
Tel: (+33) 91 919151

Nice   20 Boulevard Carabacal
              06007 Nice
              Tel: (+33) 93 559155

Paris   Chambre de Commerce de Paris
              27 Avenue de Friedland
              Paris
              Tel: (+33) 1 236 2438

Strasbourg Place Gutenburg
              67081 Strasbourg
              Tel: (+33) 88 321255

Toulouse   Palais Consulaire
              2 rue d'Alsace-Lorraine
              BP 1506
              31002 Toulouse
              Tel: (+33) 61 527200

Principle Euro Info Centres
Euroguichet
rue de la Republique 16
F-69289 Lyon Cedex 02
Tel: (+33) 78 38 1010

Euroguichet
Place St. Clement 1
BP 1004
F-57036 Metz Cedex 1
Tel: (+33) 87 33 60 00

Euroguichet
10 Place Gutenberg
F-67081 Strasbourg Cedex
Tel: (+33) 88 32 12 55

Euroguichet
Place de la Bourse 2
F-33076 Bordeaux Cedex
Tel: (+33) 56 52 65 47

Euroguichet
Centre des Salonges BP 718
16 Quai Ernest Renaud
F-44027 Nantes Cedex 04
Tel: (+33) 40 44 60 60

10
GREECE

INTRODUCTION

The Greeks are justifiably proud of their history and role as the first centre of European civilisation. This pride is reflected in their manner of doing business; they are always trustworthy, although they can be erratic. The Greek is also sometimes covert, or even insecure, which is shown in his tendency to play his cards close to his chest, keep a few tricks up his sleeve, play-act, bargain, call bluffs and generally make a business associate feel like a co-conspirator. Suspicion of the state is another trait; to the Greeks, the state is not a partner in national development, but a foe to outwit at every turn.

The Greek mentality has little preference for long-term industrial projects and is more suited to trade. Most manufacturing companies are family-owned and, although likely to have well-trained businessmen on the staff, they will still react best to business propositions put to them by people who have spent time establishing a relationship with them.

The Greek temperament is complex; the Athenian character is described by Thucydides as 'one man's success is tolerable only when others feel they could have done it themselves.' Never exert too much pressure on the Greeks; they will react at their own pace and as they see fit. The Greeks object to gross exhibition of money or personal discussion of the subject.

Greece can be many things to businessmen, the Greece, that is, of Athens and Piraeus, at any rate. It can mean engaging agents to secure for example, official approval from the relevant government ministers, and provide important liaison and formal introduction to Greek counterparts. And it can mean wonderful people and warm, lovely weather. But remember, Greece is a hard place to do business, built on a ration of who you know, and on handouts.

MAKING THE APPOINTMENT

An introduction from an acceptable institution, company or associate is the key to doing business in Greece. Where this is not immediately available, organisations such as the British Hellenic Chamber of Commerce in Athens can facilitate the introduction. This introduction can be personal or in the form of a letter to be presented at the first meeting.

Having secured an introduction, your Greek counterpart can be approached by telephone or letter to secure an appointment. The letter could be in Greek, but the Greek businessman is aware of the complexity of his language and will be prepared to accept a letter written in the mother language of the business-person. If you choose the letter route, however, beware. Greeks dislike letter-writing and may well ignore the nicety of a written response. Telephone after a couple of weeks to ensure your request has been received. You may offer an interpreter, but this may not be necessary, as Greeks generally speak good English, French and German. Greek translation is very difficult.

The role of the secretary varies in large and small companies. In large multinationals, a modern, complementary role is exercised. In small companies the boss will arrange everything in his own way. Everything that has to be done is done through him. However, the route for communication can be directly to the functional head, if he exists. It is very unlikely that an executive will react without senior discussion and reference.

THE MEETING

Once a meeting has been set up, it is best to keep the discussion formal in nature. The Greeks shake hands as frequently as most Europeans and will treat you with great courtesy, offering refreshment. Be fully prepared for the meeting and know your – and his – business well.

The Greek, if he has time, likes to get to know the person with whom he is doing business, and he may spend some time in small talk, effectively summing you up. Do not try to bring the subject back to business, as this will only antagonise him. At all times follow his lead, but do not be afraid to haggle; not only will the Greek businessman feel cheated intellectually if you accept his initial offer, he will also distrust you.

Contracts are best left to lawyers and will be explicit. The Greek, having once made the deal, will honour it, except when (and this is a dying habit) he thinks he can improve upon it for you. This improvement in specification might well be made uni-laterally, so it is wise to keep an eye on production. The Greeks will sue very quickly if your end of the contract is unfulfilled. The speed of their actions is not only driven by their own desire to be paid, but also by the Central Bank who, having given special approval for foreign currency deals (Greece still has exchange controls), want to see evidence of the business transaction as soon as possible.

Gaining an interview indicates a potential need to do a deal. It is not unknown for Greek companies to receive orders or enquiries for products which, because they are at current full capacity, will be ignored. Such is the immediacy of the Greeks that they will not even offer a letter of explanation or attempt to preserve the order for another year.

If business is successfully completed, take care in congratulating your Greek colleagues on the detail of your agreement: the Greeks will never be really sure they have struck a good deal, and reference to it will tend to raise suspicion rather than establish mutual harmony.

The Greeks are a friendly people, and even have an ancient god of hospitality to foreigners; however, do not try to break with formality too quickly.

ENTERTAINING

Business meals

Greeks eat little during the morning and early evening. The breakfast meeting does not exist in Greece, because the Greeks do not take breakfast! And they begin work at 7.00 am in the summer. Lunch is also taken late, in Athens around 3.00–3.30 pm – the end of the working day. Greeks in the provinces will go home for lunch, which will be light, and then take a siesta for two hours. In the cities, lunch may be taken in a restaurant; if this is suggested it is a sign of growing warmth in the relationship.

The main business entertainment meal is dinner. This will be taken any time from 9.00 to 9.30 pm and for those active enough can last until 2.00 am! Business may well be concluded over dinner and, if so, accept it. Congratulate your partner on a good deal and take whatever is offered in the way of hospitality.

Dining out is the preferred way of entertaining, but if you are invited home this is still further recognition of your importance. A request to join the family at the weekend must be accepted. If attending the home, flowers are appropriate or chocolates (a sign of Europeanism – both major Greek chocolate manufacturers have been recently bought out by Nestlé and Suchard).

The Greeks are far from the most punctual of people, but be on time yourself as a matter of courtesy.

Subjects for social discussion

Greeks are expansive and individual. Corporate entertainment takes on a very personal character. Small groups of businessmen might be invited to a yacht for the evening, or a weekend cruise. This, however, is difficult to distinguish from personal entertainment, and should be treated with the same respect.

Gifts

The practice of giving gifts to secure a good relationship is now almost obsolete. A good quality item which is not ostentatious would be accepted if a particularly high level of service or assistance had been given. This should not, of course, (nor should it seem to) be linked to the outcome of a particular business transaction.

Dress

Formal dress is not always important in Greece. Men will wear open-necked shirts and trousers, women dresses and skirts (women do not normally wear trousers). In senior business meetings and for most directors, lightweight business suits will be worn. Unlike many countries, the cut of your counterpart's suits will not necessarily identify his status, so do not judge him by his clothes.

WOMEN IN BUSINESS

Women are seen as a very powerful influence behind the scenes and at home. Women who graduate are usually directed towards medicine and the caring professions. In Greece today, the main role of women is still considered to be as wives and mothers, and career women are treated with suspicion.

WORKING HOURS AND PUBLIC HOLIDAYS

Athens works summer and winter times. In the summer, work begins at 7.00 am and finishes at 3.00 pm; winter hours are 7.30 am to 3.30 pm. Remember, there is no real lunch break, except for a snack break at about 10.30 am. These times change in Piraeus. Being a major international port, it is supported by staff to match Northern European, American and Japanese time zones.

Businessmen are prepared to take business calls at home, but usually only after 5.30–6.00 pm.

Public holidays are:

1st January	(New Year's Day)
6th January	(Epiphany)
25th March	(Independence Day)
1st May	(Labour Day)
15th August	(Assumption Day)
26th October	(St Dimitrius's Day (Salonica))
28th October	(Ochi (No) Day)
25th December	(Christmas Day)
26th December	(St Stephen's Day)

There are in addition three movable days, including Good Friday and Easter Monday.

LETTER-WRITING

The Greeks accept the uniqueness of their language, and are not resentful of those people who are unable to write or speak it. Letters are best written in English, as most Greeks accept this as the main business language. British letter-writing conventions should be followed. However, French and German are both popular business languages, and if previous contact has established either of these as a common tongue, use the appropriate letter-writing conventions for the language chosen. Forenames or initials may be used on the envelope, and the business card is, as always, a good indicator of how the recipient likes to be addressed.

MARKETING

The advertising industry in Greece is emerging from its infancy into adolescence, mainly due to the Government's lifting of price controls in 1985. The result has seen heavy investment by marketing-oriented firms, both local and international. The move towards liberalisation within the framework of the EC is also reflected in the move towards the launching of private and municipal radio and TV stations. The development will significantly influence advertising strategies in created segment markets, with new media research and more educated and specialised marketing people.

The socio-economic profile of Greece may be broken down into three main sectors:

Table 10.1   Socio-economic profile in Greece

	%
Upper	14
Middle	39
Lower	41

Source   Nielsen Hellas

The marketing drachma is split as follows:

Table 10.2   Marketing spend in Greece

	%
Newspapers	14
Magazines	24
Radio	6
TV	50
Posters	6

Source   Nielsen Hellas

The spend rankings by key categories are:

Table 10.3   Spend rankings in Greece

(1)	Food and drink
(2)	Toiletries
(3)	Retail
(4)	Household products
(5)	Automotive
(6)	Clothing

Source   Publicity Guide

Media

VAT at 6 per cent was introduced in January 1987. Consumer advertisements for pharmaceutical products and cigarettes are not allowed on TV or radio, nor are advertisements for toys. Cigarettes and toys are, however, allowed to be advertised in the press and outdoors. Agency commission for all media is 20 per cent. The Greek Advertising Agencies Association operates its own code of conduct for its members. For further information contact: Greek Advertising Agencies Association, 12 Ravine Street, Athens (Tel: (+30) 1 722 6990).

CONSUMER PREFERENCES/DIFFERENCES

Household spend

Purchase of household equipment in Greece is one of the lowest in EC except for stoves, fridges and deep freezers.

Greece is a relative newcomer to the EC and as such there are few comparative consumption figures available.

Financial awareness

Few Greeks have bank accounts and the penetration of credit cards is low.

Food spend

The Greeks have increased their meat consumption by nearly 10 per cent in the past 10 years. They have one of the highest levels of consumption of mutton, lamb and goat in the EC; fish is popular and is eaten as much as the total of beef, veal and pork combined.

More cheese is consumed in Greece than in any other member state although France is not far behind in percentage terms. Second only to Italy, the Greeks consume more bread and pasta products than fellow states.

Drink consumption is equally divided in volume between beer and wine.

General consumer spend

One of the lowest spend levels of penetration in Greece is on clothing.

Percentage of passenger cars sold in the second lowest in the EC.

Greece ranks after Portugal and Spain in the trend toward the introduction of international shops.

Political trends

Local issues rather than Community ones (a trend followed in a number of EC member states voting patterns) lead the Socialists (and the Communists) to loose one seat.

The voter turnout in Greece was 78 per cent.

ESTABLISHING A BUSINESS

The Greek government is currently removing the controls on

imported capital for direct investment, in line with EC currency regulations. The establishment of a business presence in Greece requires no permission from the authorities unless the planned investment is in manufacturing or incentives, in which case approval of the Ministry of National Economy is required.

A foreign enterprise may be established in Greece either as a subsidiary or as a branch. If a subsidiary is used, it is more usually an *Anonymi Eteria* (AE) or private company rather than an *Eterio Periorismensis Efthinis* (EPE) or public company.

Approval for the establishment and registration of both subsidiaries and branches must be obtained from the competent *prefecture* of the district in which the business will be located. An AE needs two shareholders (who may be foreigners) and a minimum capital of five million drachmae. The annual financial statements must be filed and, in the case of a subsidiary, published.

If a branch is set up, the foreign company must have a capital of five million drachmae if it is a corporation, or 200,000 drachmae if it is a limited liability company.

Management structure

Ownership of the smaller EPE is in the hands of 'quota holders'. No share certificates are issued, only quota certificates. The Clerk of the Court holds the registration book of quota holders. The company is managed by one or more administrators, or the founders. The administrator(s) can be appointed through the articles of association, or by a general meeting of quota holders. Once appointed, he can bind the company in contracts and, if he is appointed in the memorandum, he can only be dismissed for serious reasons by a court decision.

The larger AEs tend to be state-controlled and are managed by a board of at least three directors. They meet at least once a month and decide on matters concerning the administration and the management of the company's assets. Directors have an obligation of confidentiality when information relating to the company is given to them.

SINGLE-MARKET EFFORTS

Government

The Government's awareness campaign has been delayed, and is unlikely until the second half of 1989.

Business

The Single Market is a popular theme for after-dinner speeches at Chambers of Commerce. Awareness of 1992 is therefore high, but there is little evidence of action except among the largest, export-oriented companies. A number of sectoral organisations in the private sector have organised conferences on the Single Market.

Surveys

There have been no surveys to date.

USEFUL ADDRESSES

Sources of information and help

British Embassy
1 Ploutarchou Street
Athens GR–106 75
Tel: (+30) 1 7236211
Tlx: 216440
Fax: 301 724 1872

Department of Trade and Industry
Exports to Europe Branch
1 Victoria Street
London SW1H 0ET
Tel: 01-215 5103 (Greece desk, capital goods)
　　　01-215 4776 (Greece desk, consumer goods)

Research sources

A.C. Nielsen Hellas Ltd (annual media survey,
　ad hoc services)
2 Charokopou Street
GR–17671 Kallithea
Athens
Tel: (+30) 1 958 8771
Tlx: 219098

Addresses for advertisers

Greek Advertisers' Association
46 Venizelou Avenue
GR–17676 Kallithea
Athens
Tel: (+30) 1 958 4383

Greek Association of Advertising Agencies
12 Ravine Street
GR–11521 Athens
Tel: (+30) 1 772 6990

Chambers of Commerce

Athens   *British–Hellenic Chambers of Commerce*
                            25 Vas Sofias Avenue
                            GR–10674
                            Athens
                            Tel: (+30) 1 721 0361/721 0493

Salonica   *Chamber of Commerce*
                            Tsimiskis 27–29
                            Salonica

Principal Euro Info Centres

Euro Info Centre
Morihovon Square 1
GR–54625 Thessaloniki
Tel:(+30) 31 53 98 17

Euro Info Centre
Yenias Street 16
GR–11528 Athens
Tel: (+30) 1 770 06 54

Euro Info Centre
7 Academias
GR–10671 Athens
Tel: (+30) 1 362 7337

II
IRELAND

INTRODUCTION

Ireland advertises itself as the European capital for skilled, youthful people. Whether this is quite right is debatable, but what is true is that one of Ireland's major assets is its well-educated, mobile young workforce.

The Republic of Ireland is separate from Northern Ireland, which is part of the UK, and this fact must never be forgotten. (Discussion on the subject should only be between the Irish). The Republic itself is split between the urban areas, where the pace of life is faster, and 'the country' where the idealistic, pastoral image of Irish rural life can be a reality. The Irish have a well-developed sense of humour which they are not afraid to turn back upon themselves; the butt of their jokes are their own Kerry men.

The business language is English, although many businessmen have learned Gaelic at school and may use it in conversation with other Irish – do not be tempted to join in.

The Irish drive on the same side of the road as the British, the buildings have a similar appearance and the people speak English. They are, however, *never* to be considered English. They should be given the same attention and care as dealing with any other foreign European country. The culture is rich and already they are probably more European than the British. They fully understand the stereotype of them held by the British; slow, provincial and slightly dull: the Irish are amongst the brightest and sharpest dealers you are ever likely to meet. They are liable to take offence easily and, because of the concentration in major urban areas (particularly Dublin) you should be careful what you discuss and with whom. Dublin has been likened to the largest village in Europe and this seems to be very true, with friendship, family and education networks linking most senior executives in one way or another.

Finally, avoid the written or verbal use of the word *Eire*; although it is the Gaelic for Ireland, it is only acceptable if the sender of the letter has written it all in that language and speaks it. If written in English, a letter should be addressed to the Republic of Ireland.

MAKING THE APPOINTMENT

Initial contact by letter is expected, although the telephone call followed up by a letter is acceptable. In most major companies the secretary will hold the diary and can arrange appointments. She is one with whom to develop a rapport. In small companies, or when an introduction has been given by another Irish businessman, then a direct and informal telephone call to your counterpart is acceptable. Always confirm in writing. Letter-writing conventions are the same as in the UK.

THE MEETING

At the meeting, be prepared for a fairly informal discussion: those who enter directly into business negotiations are not looked upon favourably. The Irish will move very quickly to using first names, even at the initial meeting, and will enjoy elements of the discussion which are outside the business theme. This more social approach to business means that appointments can take much longer than planned, and your travel plans or subsequent appointments should be taken into account.

The Irish are less inclined to get into complex legal discussions, and wish to agree a deal in principle rather than be bothered, initially, with the detail. Be prepared for a change once formal proposals are submitted. They will question and seek clarification on all points, and even try to renegotiate partially at this stage, if it suits them, away from the original principles. Also, do not be fooled by their general openness and friendship. You should not drop your guard, although you should seem to take it all at face value.

You cannot be confident that a deal is secure until the documents are signed. Once this is done, the Irish are committed and will deliver. This is where the networking can work negatively: if a business transaction is poorly honoured many will know about it, which will have an adverse effect on the standing of the businessman concerned.

It is easy to make contact with senior figures in the media for PR purposes. Do not do this without a strong public relations consultant. The Irish media are among the most professional and ruthless in the world.

ENTERTAINMENT

Business meals

Breakfast meetings are becoming more common, owing largely to the American influence.

Lunch will be a normal extension of any business which occurs at that time, and is taken during 12.30–1.30 pm. The tax system has removed tax relief on lavish business entertaining, so if you invite, expect to pay. It is unlikely that an expensive lunch will be arranged; in Dublin a gentleman's club, hotel or yacht club are acceptable venues. Drinking has been cut considerably at lunchtime: expect one drink and one bottle of wine. In total, the lunch should take no more than an hour and a half.

Dinner is a wholly different event. The Irish reputation for good conversation and hospitality is fuelled by the excellence of the stout (Guinness in Dublin and Murphy's in Limerick) and the gregarious nature of the Irish. Do not be surprised to find yourself sitting next to a government minister or at least a close friend of one. It pays to know who they are in advance. In a restaurant, the true feel of an Irish village emerges, with mealtime conversation interrupted by the Irish counterpart's acknowledgement of his friends and peers. Business is usually conducted before dinner or early on; the real purpose of the meal is to evaluate people upon whom the final decision will be made. For this reason you should keep your wits about you and not get too carried away with the entertainment.

In most countries, invitations to the home convey a sense of acceptance. Ireland is no exception and if invited to a business partner's home you should certainly accept. For the hostess, flowers or chocolates are favourites and the host, because of high taxation, will appreciate duty-free spirits or wine.

Subjects for social discussion

The family, car, house and culture are the foundations of conversation. Avoid politics and religion unless asked, and even then try to remain neutral. Sport has a strong following in Ireland and a knowledge of international Irish sports personalities will impress. It is not wise to criticise the Irish, even in jest, or if they themselves initiate it; to join in can sour a relationship. Self-criticism is acceptable.

Business hospitality

This is a growing phenomenon in the Republic. It is acceptable for large Irish and international companies to support the arts and sport. Because of the scarcity of tickets for good quality sporting events, they should be accepted if at all possible. The

Irish attitude to entertaiment should be remembered, and a local hotel room booked!

At cultural events, spouses will attend and you are likely to receive an invitation for your partner. It is essential though you should take someone along.

Gifts

Initially, these are closely restricted to business-endorsed objects. However, it is possible, as your relationship develops – particularly with middle or lower management – that a bottle of duty-free spirits would be welcomed.

Dress

Convention is the key. The Irish individuality as a nation does not go as far as breaking with British conventions of dress, and adhering to these conventions will ensure no embarrassments. Women and young people as a whole dress very well and stylishly. Flamboyance is avoided, as are the excesses of female dress, such as mini skirts.

WOMEN IN BUSINESS

Women's role in commerce and industry still suffers from the restrictive stereotyping, often prevalent in Catholic countries, of women as child-raisers. Promotions will thus generally go to men, who are likely to have a more 'stable' employment record.

WORKING HOURS AND PUBLIC HOLIDAYS

Working hours in general are the same as in the UK, 9.00 am–5.30 pm, Monday to Friday. However, there is a growing tendency for executives to start early and work late, though less so than in the UK. The Irish businessman likes to separate business from family life, but is prepared to take work home and receive office calls at home. Usually holiday entitlement is four to five weeks, which will normally be taken as one main holiday in the summer.

The following are public holidays:

1st January	(New Year's Day)
17th March	(St Patrick's Day
25th December	(Christmas Day)
26th December	(Boxing Day)

There are, in addition, five movable days, including Good Friday and Easter Monday.

LETTER-WRITING

Gaelic is a live language for most Irish people, although none will expect to conduct business in it. In almost every case, a letter following UK conventions will be appropriate.

MARKETING

The main media operative in Ireland include RTE (radio and television), both operating a two-channel service, and the national press which currently consists of four daily, three evening and four Sunday papers, backed by the provincial press. Growth areas are outdoor advertising and exhibitions. Direct response has lagged behind the rest of Europe, but changes in the An Post (Post Office) should encourage greater use. Radio is of particular significance in the Irish market, holding an estimated 12 per cent of advertising, due mainly to the fact that state radio has always carried commercials.

The socio-economic breakdown is similar to that of the UK and uses the same definitions, with the addition of two categories: F50− and F50+ which denote farmers who own more or less than 50 acres.

Table 11.1   Socio-economic breakdown in the Republic of Ireland

	%
AB	9
C₁	20
C₂	22
D	22
E	7
F50−	10
F50+	10

Source   JNMR

The media pound is spent in the following way:

Table 11.2 Media spend in Ireland

	%
Newspapers	34
Magazines	9
TV	37
Radio	12
Outdoor	8

Source   ASI

The spend rankings by key categories are:

Table 11.3   Key spend rankings in Ireland

(1) Food, dairy products and confectionery
(2) Financial
(3) Motor trade
(4) Alcoholic beverages
(5) Personal hygiene
(6) Agriculture
(7) Clothing

Source   ASI

Media

All media advertising is subject to VAT at 25 per cent, but can
be reclaimed as a legitimate expense by registered advertisers.
Agency commission is 15 per cent for magazines, 12.5 per cent
for most national newspapers and 15 per cent for broadcast
media. Advertising of cigarettes and spirits is not permitted on
TV, radio or in the cinema. A code of advertising standards for
Ireland lists a range of products for which there are restrictions
and special recommendations. There is also a special code for
radio and TV. For more information, contact: Advertising
Standards Authority for Ireland, IPC House, 35/39 Shelbourne
Road, Dublin 4 (Tel: 0001 608766); and for radio and TV: RTE,
Donnybrooke, Dublin 4 (Tel: 0001 693111).

CONSUMER PREFERENCES/DIFFERENCES

Household spend

Although the Irish, *per capita*, spend less on consumption of
durables, food, etc, than most of the EC member states, there are
a few areas where the spend percentage is high. One of those
areas is on the household. More specifically, there is a growing
trend in purchasing of electrical household goods.

Financial awareness

All the major international banks have a presence in Dublin.
Although penetration by credit cards is not high. One of the
causes could be that there is a noticeable age gap (20 to 40 year
olds) in Ireland's human resources.

The Irish Government is trying to encourage international
finance houses to open offices in Ireland in preparation for

1992. It will be interesting to see what market penetration, if any, this may have on the home community.

Food spend

Ireland's consumption records for food are in potatoes and beer. It is one of the few countries in the Community where a sizeable volume of tea is drunk.

Meat consumption in Ireland ranks sixth in the Community with a market share of 1.15 per cent. Roughly speaking, the Irish consume equal amounts of all the main meat products. Although they eat relatively low levels of cheese, the Irish are the second highest consumers of butter in the Community.

General consumer spend

The lowest number of cars is sold in Ireland. But the Japanese presence in car sales represents as much as 40 per cent.

Clothes also have a low spend priority in Ireland and again this can relate to the human resource problem.

Political trends

With Ireland holding her national elections on the same day as the Euro elections (as in Greece), voter reaction was bound to be somewhat clouded by local rather than EC issues. Both Fianna Fail and Fine Gael lost two seats each. Ireland has a total of 15 Euro seats.

ESTABLISHING A BUSINESS

It is not necessary to obtain approval from the Irish Government before setting up a business in Ireland, although exchange-control requirements must be satisfied.

A foreign company may operate in Ireland either by establishing an Irish subsidiary, usually a private company, or a branch.

Every Irish company, and an overseas company establishing a place of business in Ireland, must submit its memorandum of association (charter) and articles of association (by-laws), translated into English where necessary, together with certain other particulars to the Registrar of Companies. Irish limited liability companies must file audited financial statements each year. It is not permissable for a corporation to be a director of an Irish incorporated company.

Business may also be conducted in Ireland through a partnership. If this is the case, the income will be taxed in the hands of the individual partners. Although unusual, it is also possible for a trust to trade in Ireland. However, trading trusts are subject to income tax at the rate of 35 per cent and are also liable for a 20 per cent surcharge on undistributed income of the trust.

Most Irish companies are private companies, that is they have less than 50 members and there are certain restrictions as to the transfer of shares or debentures. There is no minimum amount of share capital, but there must be at least two shareholders. Where such companies wish to receive government grants, the government body will normally request that there is a certain level of shareholders' equity in the company. They generally insist that an amount of equity, in the form of either share capital or subordinated loan, equal to the amount of grants received, must be injected into the company.

Management structure

For private companies, the memorandum and articles of association give the company structure (no qualifications are needed). By law, all companies must have two directors and a secretary. The directors can have wide powers of decision-making, and many articles are written to restrict this power in favour of the shareholders. There is no legal requirement for board meetings, but any director can call a meeting which must be held, provided sufficient notice is given. Decisions at board level are taken by majority vote, with a quorum of directors being two.

Employee representation for public and private companies is a matter for local negotiation; there is no legal requirement. Worker participation does exist at board level in some state industries. As in private companies, the actual internal structure of the company's management is a matter for internal rules. The same basic legal requirements apply to private as well as to public companies.

SINGLE-MARKET EFFORTS

Government

A campaign, 'European', was launched on 4 July 1988. A basic information booklet was produced, and also factsheets on specific sectors. An information hotline 'Freefone European Market 1992' has also been established.

Business

Ireland has set up an international Financial Services Centre at Customs House Docks, Dublin. This has been created to attract European and non-European organisations allowing them a base when selling into the European financial markets. It is hoped that companies will be attracted by favourable corporation tax treatment.

Surveys

No survey information is available.

USEFUL ADDRESSES

Sources of information and help

Irish Embassy
14 Three Kings Yard
Davies Street
London W1Y 2EH
Tel: 01-629 8200
Tlx: 23520

Research sources

Market Research Bureau of Ireland Ltd
  (consumer research, media research)
MRBI House
43 Northumberland Avenue
Dun Laoghaire
Co. Dublin
Tel: (+0001) 804661

Addresses for advertisers

Advertising Standards Authority for Ireland
IPC House
35/39 Shelbourne Road
Dublin 4
Tel: (+0001) 608766

Association of Advertisers in Ireland
44 Lower Leeson Street
Dublin 2
Tel: (+0001) 761016

Institute of Advertising Practitioners in
    Ireland
35 Upper Fitzwilliam Street
Dublin 2
Tel: (0001) 764876
Tlx: 93381

Chamber of Commerce
Dublin   7 Clare Street
Dublin 2
Tel: (+0001) 686633

Principal Euro Info Centres
European Business Information Centre
Merrion Hall
PO Box 203
Strand Road
Sandymont
Dublin 4
Tel: (+0001) 169 5011

European Business Information Centre
The Granary
Michael Street
Limerick
Tel: (+353) 61 40777

12
ITALY

INTRODUCTION

After Greece, Italy could surely claim to be the epicentre of western culture, with its great cities of Rome, Florence and Venice. However, until recently Italy tended to be a fragmented country, lacking in the national consciousness of most other major European nations.

The rise in Italy's economic standing (in GDP terms, Italy ranks behind Germany and France, but close to or above the UK) has given birth to a new nationalism. This performance has been achieved in the swing away from fascism since the Second World War.

Italy has a North/South divide, demarcated just south of Rome. Milan, in the industrialised North, is the centre of business and, according to Northern Italians, sophistication as well. The Southerners, with Neapolitans as a prime example, tend to be more relaxed in their outlook and less speedy in their business transactions. However, the volatile Italian temperament seems to transcend regional differences! The Italians use their whole bodies in communication, gesticulating widely with their arms and shoulders.

Punctuality is not a feature of Italian behaviour, but making unilateral decisions to change or cancel appointments is. When dealing with Italians it is you, not them, who must adjust to a different tempo and culture. They are easily offended and excited, but tend to have an impersonal approach to business. If quick decisions are required, expect to wait until the very last moment, and, if government departments are involved in your negotiations, allow plenty of time, since bureaucratic transactions take a very long time and patience is always necessary. Insistence can also be important: in the country of Machiavelli, much can be done to restrict the progression of unwanted, but officially allowable, decisions.

The young are the driving force in Italy, bringing the country into line with European trends. The word 'yuppie' has been incorporated into the vocabulary, and the consumer-spend mentality that category represents is an index of modern Italian society.

Italians are distinguished from other Europeans by the singular use of their language, coupled with their zest for life. Hand-shaking is extensively used and an attempt to speak and write their language is almost universally appreciated.

MAKING THE APPOINTMENT

Write early for an appointment and make sure, if possible, that the letter is in good Italian. In this initial communication, express the purpose of your meeting, giving as much detail as you can. You should allow your Italian counterpart time to respond to you and to make an appointment. However, Italians are not great letter-writers and, if you have not heard within three to four weeks of writing, then a telephone call to your contact's secretary will help.

The Italian's use of a secretary's skills varies. In large multinationals secretaries will be used to their full capacity; in smaller companies only their typing will be in demand. You will be able to identify in what capacity your particular counterpart's secretary acts by her ability to make the appointment on behalf of her boss. You may need to insist on speaking to him directly. Use facsimile if you are unable to make contact verbally.

Once the appointment is fixed, reconfirm a week or so before leaving home, and again the day before the meeting is due to take place. Italians move their diary appointments to suit themselves, and do not always feel the need to inform those who are not part of their day's plans. You should make sure that you are accompanied by those who have the skills to progress business matters; engineers, marketing men and interpreters. (You should offer in your letter to bring an interpreter, if necessary.) Be on time, and be patient.

THE MEETING

The volatile character of the Italians, together with their often impersonal approach to business, can make them difficult negotiating partners. Add to this the fact that they will usually be impeccably dressed, immaculately groomed, and work from well-appointed offices, and the prospect can be quite daunting.

In the first meeting much time will be spent in deciding whether the company wishes to do business with you. (In other words, they will be summing you up.) Go at the Italians' pace, oiling the wheels of communication with appropriate compliments. Italians are probably among the best at delivering a disparaging remark in the most charming way. Do not let them get away with this; respond with the same level of wit, eloquence and charm. Italians respect those who compete and win on their own terms. At all times, retain a calm exterior and do not react to any momentary change in your host's moods.

ENTERTAINING

Business meals

Italians are great lovers of good food, and will usually be happy for lunch or dinner to form part of the business transaction. Breakfast is a small meal in Italy, consisting of coffee and rolls. It is also taken early, and so makes a poor opportunity for business transactions. Working breakfasts are also perceived to be very American – not a positive attribute.

Lunch, on the other hand, will be costly in food and time. An invitation to lunch or dinner should be accepted; not to do so would be seen as ungracious. If you have more than one meeting during the morning, bear in mind Italian timekeeping and check out the prospects of business entertainment. The Italians are experts on food and enjoy opportunities for hospitality, so let them choose the restaurant and compliment them on the food served.

Wine will be plentiful, but your Italian colleague will not take offence if you do not drink at his pace; and if you cannot, you should not try!

Dinner appointments are offered less regularly than lunch, are taken at around 9.00 pm, and suggest progression in the negotiations. Initially, the meal is likely to be taken at a restaurant favoured by your counterpart, where his local presence will be recognised and commented upon. Whoever issued the invitation should offer to pay, but don't be surprised if Italians insist. A little resistance would be considered good manners, but give in gracefully and quickly. If you should be invited home to meet the family, this is a sign of good progress in your relationship. A small gift to the hostess is expected. This may be wine (make sure it is Italian, and recognisably good), flowers or chocolates. Small gifts for the children, if they are of an appropriate age, would be appreciated.

Subjects for social discussion

The Italians are very proud of their families, and complimenting them and enjoying their successes are good discussion topics.

Overt pride in (but not comparison with) your own family is also very acceptable.

Business hospitality

As in most European countries, this is used much less than in the UK. Personally arranged events are a great deal more common. An invitation to spend some time at the summer house should, if at all possible, be accepted.

Gifts

Generosity is a national trait which Italians share with other Mediterranean countries. Gifts outside the business transaction might well be made and, if not seen as an immediate response, will be appreciated. The Italians like to give stylish gifts which have fairly high value, so make sure, if you are giving business gifts, that they represent the quality of your company.

Dress

Style emerges through all of the Italians' dealing, and their dress is no exception. The Italians are proud of their fashion designers and men are exceptionally well groomed on almost all occasions. Conservative, well-cut suits, shirts and ties should be chosen. It is acceptable to remove tie and jacket, but wait upon an invitation from your host or, if he is already so dressed, ask permission. If you are going to remove your designer jacket, make sure you are wearing a designer shirt, too! Women dress well, but not flamboyantly. Good shoes are an important part of an Italian's wardrobe.

WOMEN IN BUSINESS

Women are becoming more accepted in the service industries and commerce. There is still considerable male chauvinism, particularly in industrial companies and in the South. Italians will be charming, but expect to have a decision referred back to a male decision-maker. Women should not be surprised at this, and may have to ease their Italian colleagues into a new understanding.

WORKING HOURS AND PUBLIC HOLIDAYS

Business usually starts early, around 8.00–9.00 am, and a long break is taken at about one o'clock. Work recommences at about 4.00 pm, and continues into the early evening, finishing between 7.00 and 8.00 pm. The Italians enjoy their holidays which are, on average, four or five weeks, taken in one long break in the summer months, usually August. This will normally be spent with the extended family unit.

Public holidays are:

1st January	(New Year's Day)
25th April	(Liberation Day)
1st May	(Labour Day)
15th August	(Assumption)
1st November	(All Saints' Day)
8th December	(Immaculate Conception)
25th December	(Christmas Day)
26th December	(St Stephen's Day)

There is, in addition, Easter Monday, which is movable.

LETTER-WRITING

The envelope

English	Italian
Mr	Egregio Signor (initials, surname), or
	Egr Sig* (initials, surname)
Mrs	Gentile Signora (initials, surname), or
	Gent ma Sig ra (initials, surname)
Miss	Gentile Signorina (initials, surname), or
	Gent ma Sig na (initials, surname)

Salutation

	Letter written in:
Italian	English
Egregio Signor (Surname)	Dear Mr (Surname), or
	Dear Signor (Surname)
Gentile Signora (Surname)	Dear Mrs (Surname), or
	Dear Signora (Surname)
Gentile Signorina (Surname)	Dear Miss (Surname), or
	Dear Signorina (Surname)
Egregio Signor	Dear Sir
Egregio Signori	Dear Sirs

Closing

Individual	Distinti Saluti, or	Yours sincerely
	La prego di gradire i	
	miei piu cordiali saluti	
Company	Distinti saluti	Yours faithfully

Note
*It is the custom to abbreviate titles, but only on the envelope. The first forename may be used in place of an initial.

MARKETING

The Italian media industry has recently undergone two major changes. The first is due to an upswing, since 1983, of the Italian economic climate, and the second was caused by wide-ranging government legislation. For instance, in the press sector since 1988 there is no longer fixed pricing for newspaper sales, and the Government has stopped financially supporting the daily press.

Other changes include the improvement in distribution and a participation in the Europe-wide growth in magazine titles. Italian television is not known for its quality programming, but is famed for its 'stripping housewives'. It has over 350 local channels, but only three state-owned channels. Television is thought to have played an important part in unifying the country within its new national consciousness by highlighting the similarities of different regions rather than their differences.

Socio-economically, the country is broken down into four main segments:

Table 12.1   Socio-economic grading in Italy

	%
Upper/upper middle	10.7
Middle	46.9
Middle/lower	34.6
Lower	7.8

Source   ISPI

The marketing lira is spent in the following ways:

Table 12.2   Marketing spend in Italy

	%
Newspapers	22.0
Magazines	19.2
TV	49.5
Radio	3.6
Cinema	0.3
Outdoor	5.4

Source   ASSAP

The spend rankings by key categories are:

Table 12.3   Key categories spend in Italy

(1)	Food
(2)	Toiletries, healthcare
(3)	Automotive
(4)	Beverages
(5)	Mass media
(6)	Clothing and fabrics
(7)	Household cleaners

Source   NASA

Media

VAT is levied on all media at 18 per cent. Tobacco advertising is forbidden on all media. Alcoholic beverages and a large number of other products are subject to restrictions on state TV, whilst advertisements for the following are not allowed: contraceptives, weapons and accessories, products and treatments for physical development, gambling houses and horse-race betting halls, betting contests and lotteries (except those organised on behalf of public organisations), moneylenders and companies offering loans (except public banks or public financial institutions), fortune-tellers and the like, matrimonial agencies and correspondence clubs, employment agencies and bureaux, private investigation agencies, undertakers, entertainments restricted to adults and newspapers of political organisations.

Apart from tobacco advertising, independent TV has no advertising restrictions. For further information, contact: SACIS, via Tomacelli 139, Rome (Tel: (+39) 639 6841).

CONSUMER PREFERENCES/DIFFERENCES

Household spend

The Italians are spending more on their home although their priority is still on the purchase of food rather than on household equipment and appliances. Indeed, they have one of the lowest spends on home electrical appliances.

The breakdown of household spending on domestic goods and services is as follows.

Table 12.4   Italian household spend

Items	%
Furniture (including carpets and other floor coverings)	28
White goods	12
Furnishings	9
Table utensils	6
Domestic and other household services	45

Source   Eurostat/Mintel

Financial awareness

The Italians have a fairly low level of banking use. This trend is also followed in the penetration of credit cards, which is low.

Food spend

Food and drink play a large part in Italian life. The Italians consume more pasta and bread than any other country in the EC. They also have the highest percentage of consumption of fish *per capita*. Equal amounts of beef, veal, pork and poultry are eaten.

Italy is a wine producing nation and wine consumption is high, second only to that in France. Comparatively little beer is drunk.

General consumer spend

Of all the EC member states, the Italians have the most inward-looking regard to the purchase of their cars, for example, Fiat have over 60 per cent of the home market. The Italians have the second highest level of passenger car purchase in the EC.

The highest priority for the Italian single man is his preference for spending on clothes. As far as men's clothes are concerned the Italian male spends more money on his stylish looks than on his cars or motorcycles. This trend is not followed by the women although recently there has been an increase in their spending levels with regard to clothes.

Political trends

With a total of 81 Euro seats at stake, the Italian electorate proved that their interest in what happens in the EC was still very much alive. Italy recorded the third highest turnout of voters (82 per cent). The Green Party showed the most gain winning five seats. This was their first election in Italy.

ESTABLISHING A BUSINESS

Foreign investors are free to adopt any of the forms of business entity available to Italian citizens. All companies and other entities established in Italy, even if by foreign investors, are governed by the Italian Civil Code, and there is no particular law concerning foreign investment. Special laws apply to banks, insurance companies, holding and trust companies. All new enterprises must register their establishment at the local court and Chamber of Commerce, notify the local tax office and, if staff are employed, register with the National Social Security Institute.

Companies that intend to import or export goods subject to licensing procedures must register with the Ministry of Foreign Trade, and all retailers (including suppliers of food and drink, mail order and vending machine operators) must be specially licensed by the municipal, or sometimes regional, authorities.

The minimum capital required for a *Società per Azioni (SpA)* – public (joint stock) company – is Lit 200,000,000. For a private (limited liability) company – *Società a responsabilità limitata (Srl)* – the minimum capital is Lit 20,000,000. The capital is represented by quotas, each having a minimum par value of Lit 1,000. Subscriptions can be made in cash and 'in kind'. 'Pay-in-kind' is restricted, and must be of property with an economic value.

Management structure

The governing bodies of an *SpA* are the shareholders in general meeting, the directors and the statutory auditors. Management is entrusted to a sole director or Board of Directors; the latter may contain both executives and independent members. The size of the Board is determined by the provisions of the company's Articles of Association. The chairman of the board must be elected by the directors or the shareholders; normally directors need not be Italian citizens or residents and they need not be shareholders. Directors are liable to the company for any failure to fulfil their duties, and may be liable to shareholders or third parties who are harmed by the director's actions, neglect or fraudulent behaviour.

There is a Board of Statutory Auditors (*Sindaci*) numbering some three or five persons; members are not required to be Italian citizens and must not be employees or directors (or close relatives of directors of the company.

According to the law, the statutory auditors are responsible for ensuring that the law and the articles of association are respected and the company's accounting records are properly kept. In addition, the statutory auditors are responsible for the quarterly checking of the company's cash in hand and the existence of investments, the examination and approval of the annual balance sheet, and the valuation of the company's assets.

As with an SpA, directors of an Srl have the power to represent and bind the company in business. Statutory audits do not apply unless the company's capital exceeds lira 100,000,000.

At present, there are no legal requirements to institute works councils, or to include employees' representatives on Boards of Directors. However, a workers' committee (*consiglio di fabbrica*) is usually established, the number of members of which depends on the size of the company concerned. This committee is entitled to information concerning the company's economic situation, sales, production and employment.

SINGLE-MARKET EFFORTS

Government
The 'National Council for the Single Market' was formally launched on 9 December 1988 as part of a package including the establishment of a telephone hotline and a database on 'European Integration'.

Business
A number of seminars and conferences have been held involving trades unions, political parties, traders' groups, etc. The larger industrial concerns are drawing up and implementing revised corporate plans for 1992.

Surveys
There is no information available at the present time.

USEFUL ADDRESSES

Sources of information and help

Italian Chamber of Commerce for Great Britain
Walmer House
Regent Street
London W1
Tel: 01-637 3153
Tlx: 269096 ITACAM G

British Chamber of Commerce for Italy
Via Agnello 8
I-20124 Milan
Tel: (+39) 2 876981
Tlx: 332490 BRITAL I

Research sources

A.C. Nielsen Company
Via Dante 7
I-20123 Milan
Tel: (+39) 2 85621
Tlx: 3340591

Doxa (member of the Gallup organisation)
Galleria San Carlo 6,
I-20122 Milan
Tel: (+39) 2 790871
Tlx: 335161 DOXA I

Addresses for advertisers

SACIS (for details of advertising legislation)
Via Tomacelli 139,
Rome
Tel: (+39) 6 396841

Associazione Italiana delle Agenzie di Pubblicita a Servicio Completo (advertising association)
Via Larga 19
I-20122 Milan
Tel: (+39) 2 802086

Chambers of Commerce

Florence   P. dei Giudici 3
             Florence
             Tel: (+39) 55 27951

Genoa	Genoa Chamber of Commerce Via Garibaldi 4 Genoa Tel: (+39) 10 12094
	Chamber of Commerce for Foreign Trade P. Banchi Genoa Tel: (+39) 10 208864
Milan	Milan Chamber of Commerce Via Meravigli 9B Milan Tel: (+39) 2 88541
	Chamber of Commerce for International Exchange Via 18 Gennaio Milan Tel: (+39) 2 2719288
	International Chamber of Commerce Via Cordusio 2 Milan Tel: (+39) 2 802517
Naples	Naples Chamber of Commerce P. Bovio Naples Tel: (+39) 81 206761
	Chamber of Commerce for International Exchange Via Flavio Gioia 4 Naples Tel: (+39) 81 310347
Rome	Via de 'Burro' 147 Rome Tel: (+39) 6 679 4541
Turin	Via San Frencesco da Paola 24 Turin Tel: (+39) 11 57161
Venice	Via XXII Marzo 2032 San Marco Venice Tel: (+39) 41 703499

Principal Euro Info Centres

Eurosportello
Via delle Orsole 4/b
I-20143 Milan
Tel: (+39) 2 154456

Eurosportello
Via Ciprol
I-25124 Brescia
Tel: (+39) 30 222172

Eurosportello
Corso Meridionale 58
I-80143 Naples
Tel: (+39) 81 269897

Eurosportello
Via San Domenica 4
I-40124 Bologna
Tel: (+39) 51 529611

13
LUXEMBOURG

INTRODUCTION

The importance of Luxembourg as one of the founder countries of the EEC has little to do with its size or its population, which is the smallest of all the member states. Luxembourg, like many smaller countries of the European Community, has maintained its importance to the Community by using what resources it has to create a role for itself. For Luxembourg this derives from its geographical positioning. Quite literally, it is at the heart of Europe. Owing more to its German rather than French neighbours, it now has three official languages: French, German and Luxembourgish. French is the most popular language in use, and today the country is culturally more tied to France than to Germany.

In 1921 a convention of Economic Union was signed between Luxembourg and Belgium. This created a customs-free zone, and gave Luxembourg and Belgium fiscal parity with one another.

The small population (367,000) is supplemented by many foreign businesses, but the lack of a firm national character has led the Luxembourger to be somewhat distant and sensitive about his nation. For this reason, Luxembourgers jealously guard their separate identity, and should by no means be considered as vaguely French, German or Belgian. In general, Luxembourgers are friendly and like to show off their language skills; they appreciate attempts to use the Luxembourg dialect for simple greetings and thank-yous.

Luxembourg is not renowned for its exciting lifestyle, although this may change as it becomes recognised as the major European centre of banking and investment fund management. Luxembourg's prominence comes from its realistic taxation on investment income, and this is where it proposes to be at the centre of Europe in more ways than geographically.

MAKING THE APPOINTMENT

It is best, in the first instance, to send a letter to an organisation in Luxembourg in order to arrange a visit. English is well understood in commerce, but as French is the main language it would be wise to use French for the business transaction, provided you have a working knowledge of that language. Offers of an interpreter at any meeting would be well received, but may not always be necessary.

The role of the secretary is rather more formal also, but is more in the French style with large multinationals using all the secretarial skills and small businesses and professionals using just typing skills. Regardless of her immediate ability to help (she may not have the boss's diary), the secretary is to be won over and respected, as she can play an influential role in securing subsequent interviews.

THE MEETING

The European practice of handshaking is much in evidence in Luxembourg business practice. The business environment tends to be very formal, with addressing by surname retained for much longer than is usually the case elsewhere.

The first meeting will be held in the company's office and it is very important to be on time. As well as being formal in his outlook, the Luxembourger is fastidious in his business ways. Regardless of whether the business interview is with commerce or government (government offices stay open to 6.00 pm, commercial offices are open usually until 5.00 pm), expect a very traditional atmosphere, particularly if your business counterpart is over fifty. Here, old social structures of titles and appropriately-styled respect are still required to give a good impression.

ENTERTAINING

Business meals

The breakfast meeting is not very common in Luxembourg and lunch is by no means an automatic follow-on if the time is right.

Lunch is a sure sign of progression in the interview; it will be quite short and in a good quality restaurant but it is unlikely that you will be offered lunch at home. If you extend the invitation, let him choose the location and you pay. Entertaining can be very expensive. However, because of the small size of the country, business hospitality is not usually ostentatious and is most likely to take the form of dinner, with perhaps a visit to a nightclub afterwards.

Dinner is likely to be taken outside the family home, and only business associates will attend; even this is an important sign of the building of a successful rapport. If you should be invited to dinner at home, flowers should be taken for the lady of the house and a bottle of wine for the host is acceptable. At all times remain formal in your dealings; take your cue from your host as to when to become more relaxed.

Subjects for social discussion

So far as small talk is concerned, Luxembourgers are usually happy to talk about their families. They are especially proud of their cars which they see as highly prestigious.

An understanding of the history and culture of Luxembourg is much appreciated, as it confirms your recognition of the distinct status of their country. Very little corporate entertainment is done, except perhaps at the trade fair which is held twice yearly.

Luxembourg is a very European, and small, nation. It has boundaries with Belgium, France and West Germany, and takes interest in the current affairs of all these countries. However, Luxembourgers are proud of their own national identity and topics of discussion that relate to the development of their own language and culture are popular. Do not draw too many similarities, and in particular with Belgium.

Business hospitality

Because of the size of the country and its population, opportunities to be lavish are limited. As mentioned before, the more likely routes are the one-to-one meetings with relaxing dinners and night-clubs to follow.

Gifts

So far as business gifts are concerned, the acceptable practices of most Northern European Community states apply here. Gifts should not be too lavish.

Dress

Formality is best. It is expected that conservative suits, shirts and ties should be worn on most business occasions. For women, smart, conventional clothes are the norm; trousers should not be worn.

WOMEN IN BUSINESS

Women play an ever-increasing role in Luxembourg's business life. They are generally well-educated, but the growth of their role follows the slow path adopted by most Community states. However Luxembourg tends, on the whole, to be male-oriented and although women are encouraged to take part in business, there is a male chauvinism which permeates the business community. The employment of women is most widespread in the service industries.

WORKING HOURS AND PUBLIC HOLIDAYS

Normal working hours are between 8.30 am and 12.00 am in the morning, and 2.00–5.30 pm in the afternoon. On average Luxembourgers have four weeks annual holiday.

The following are public holidays:

1st January	(New Year's Day)
1st May	(Labour Day)
23rd June	(National Day)
15th August	(Assumption)
1st November	(All Saints' Day)
2nd November	(All Souls' Day)
25th/26th December	(Christmas Day)

In addition, there are four movable days, including Easter.

LETTER-WRITING

For a letter which is written in French see pages 88-89; and for a letter in German see pages 192-193.

MARKETING

The marketing infrastructure of Luxembourg is underdeveloped compared to the structure found in its Community partners. The following is a summary of its content.

At the present time there is no consumer media or sector spends available for comparison. There are, for instance, only 250,000 radios and 150,000 television sets in the whole of the Grand Duchy. *Radio-Tele Luxembourg* operates four radio and three TV stations, broadcasting nationally.

As far as newspapers are considered, there are six daily newspapers, of which *Luxembourger Wort* or *La Voix du Luxembourg* (printed in German and French) are considered to be the main national papers. The French paper *Le Republicain Lorrain* has a large Luxembourg section and therefore has its own readership following.

CONSUMER PREFERENCES/DIFFERENCES

Very little data is available on the preferences of consumers in Luxembourg. Data is usually combined with that of the Belgian consumer. What does emerge is that Luxembourgers spend highly on their home, both furnishings and appliances. Clothes are also considered important with the more conservative of foreign designers selling well in that market.

The food consumption in Luxembourg ranks highly, *per capita*, with the rest of the community. Large quantities of pork in various forms, for example, sausages, ham, fresh meat, etc, are sold.

Harmonisation of car tax (VAT) could affect car sales as Luxembourg has one of the lowest levels of VAT (12 per cent) in the Community.

Political trends

The citizens of Luxembourg again showed how keenly aware they are of their role in selecting their representatives in Strasbourg. Luxembourg has the second highest turnout of voters in the EC showing 87 per cent. Of that, the Christian Democrats still hold three out of Luxembourg's total of six Euro seats.

ESTABLISHING A BUSINESS

Every commercial and industrial enterprise must obtain a government licence to trade. This licence will be granted only if the individual responsible produces certificates of good conduct and solvency and (with some exceptions) evidence of appropriate qualifications. These can be proved by submitting a relevant diploma or a certificate of practical experience in the trade concerned. The period of experience required varies from three months to three years. If the activity is to be exercised by a corporate body, these conditions must be fulfilled by the director or manager in charge.

A written application for a licence must be send to the Ministry for Small and Medium-Sized Businesses, in the case of a commercial undertaking, or the Ministry of Economy, in the case of an industrial undertaking. Banks and insurance companies must obtain the approval of the Ministry of Finance.

There are two types of company: the *Société à Responsabilité Limitée (SARL)* – the private company; and *Société Anonyme (SA)* – the public company. Both are governed by the same legal framework, with the difference occurring in the type of shares issued and the capital requirements. For instance, SARLs do not have conventional shares, but '*parts sociales*' and the minimum capitalisation is LF 100,000, whereas SAs have a full range of share options and a minimum capitalisation of LF 1,250,000.

Within one month of starting up, every enterprise must register basic information concerning itself, such as constitution documents and names of directors, managers and statutory auditors, with the *Administration de l'Enregistrement et des Domaines*, and file this information in the Register of Commerce (*Registre de Commerce*) kept at the District Court for the area in which the legal address of the enterprise is located. The Register of Commerce provides a copy for publication in the Official Gazette. Any changes in this information must be registered and filed in the same way, within one month of the change. Small filing fees are payable.

Every business entity is required to join the Chamber of Commerce, to which a subscription, based on profit, is payable. Enterprises having an activity subject to VAT must inform the appropriate office of the *Administration de l'Enregistrement*. The authorities collecting direct taxes such as income tax and municipal business tax must be informed, as must the Social Security Office.

Management structure

Management of the corporation is vested in a board of directors consisting of at least three members (nine, if employees can appoint directors to represent them). The directors need not be Luxembourg citizens or residents, or shareholders of the corporation.

The Board of Directors is responsible for the management of the corporation, although day-to-day management can be delegated to one or several directors or managers.

If an SA company employs at least 1,000 persons (and in some other special cases), one-third of its directors must be designated by the employees, including manual workers. The conditions of all directors' appointments, discharges and duties are determined by the articles of association, whether the directors are appointed by shareholders or employees.

Any SA employing at least 150 persons must set up a works council (*comité mixte d'entreprise*) composed of an equal number of management representatives and employees' representatives. The works council participates in decisions concerning welfare, health and safety, employee selection and evaluation and similar matters. It has the right to be informed and consulted on working conditions and significant economic matters. If the SA has 15 or more employees, then it must have employee delegates (*délégations du personnel*). These delegates hold at least six meetings per year, three of which are with the management. Delegates can only be dismissed in exceptional circumstances.

SINGLE-MARKET EFFORTS

Government

Six working groups were established to examine the impact of the Single Market on different sectors of the economy. Action is expected to follow from the groups' reports. No briefing material has been produced to date. No business initiatives or survey information are currently available.

USEFUL ADDRESSES

Chamber of Commerce

Luxembourg   7 rue Alcide de Gaspert
BP 1503
L-2981 Kirchberg
Luxembourg
Tel: (+352) 43 58 53

Principal Euro Info Centre

Euroguichet
7 rue Alcide de Gaspert
BP 1503
L-2981 Kirchberg
Luxembourg
Tel: (+352) 43 58 53

14
THE NETHERLANDS

INTRODUCTION

The Dutch, the middle-men of Europe, long ago established themselves as excellent traders, good negotiators and financially sound businesspeople. They have a commercial relationship with the UK dating back before the sixteenth century. Indeed, the first Anglo-Dutch Chamber of Commerce was set up in 1891. The Dutch also share similar tastes and attitudes with the British.

The Dutch business acumen is evident in its major international organisations; companies such as Philips, Shell and Unilever. Carrying the Community's stereotyping of thriftiness and ruthlessness in business, the Dutch have perhaps contributed more to the spirit of a United Europe than any other member nation.

Dutch society mirrors Britain to some extent, since it has a royal family and a Parliament – though the Dutch Parliament is elected by proportional representation. Like most nations, the Dutch are proud of their history and cultural achievements; unlike most, however, they have developed the ethos of foreign language, and as well as their native Dutch (little-used elsewhere in the world) most businesspeople speak English and at least one other European language – most likely French or German. The Dutch mastery of foreign languages is well proven by the following table:

Table 14.1   Mastery of language

Country	Total speaking at least one language	one language	Speaking at least two languages	three languages
	%	%	%	%
Netherlands	70.7	28.7	31.7	10.3
Belgium	43.6	22.4	15.5	5.7
Germany	39.5	32.8	6.0	0.7
France	32.6	26.0	6.0	0.7
UK	25.4	20.0	4.7	0.7

Figures produced by the World Economic Forum also rank the Netherlands high in terms of the country's political stability and successful labour relations.

To summarise a recent Netherlands Chamber of Commerce report:

> '1992 will not harmonise cultural aspects. Europe will remain fragmented regarding: language, taste, attitudes and business practice. It is here that the Dutch will benefit from the skills of international marketing and sales, transport and distribution.'

A further advantage for the Dutch is that they can reach any of the major economic centres in Europe within one day's surface travel.

MAKING AN APPOINTMENT

In all dealings with the Dutch, your overriding concerns must be punctuality, straightforwardness and lack of pretension. The Dutch Chamber of Commerce takes a leading role in making contacts in the Netherlands and should be used for the initial contact.

Once given a name, it is acceptable to telephone. The telephone call for an appointment should be confirmed by a letter. This should be concise, informative and provide all the information the Dutch counterpart will need to join you in discussions. Write to the person you wish to see, and by name; not to do so is considered very rude.

The secretary's role is similar to that in the UK: the larger the company, the more likely she is to hold the diary and be aware of the importance of your visit. She and your counterpart should be addressed with the maximum, at least initially, of formality and British good manners.

The content of your letter should always offer an interpreter by way of admission of lack of linguistic skill in Dutch (usually rejected because of the large number of English-speaking executives) and information about any advisers attending. Do not turn up with advisers unexpectedly, as this tactic may well antagonise your counterpart and so remove any advantage you may have gained.

THE MEETING

The Dutch way of conducting business will mean first, that if he agrees to see you he is 'interested' in your proposal and second that the meeting will be quite short (maximum 30–45 minutes).

This would equate to an hour or an hour-and-a-half meeting in the UK.

An important cultural point to check when dealing is the use of numbers in Dutch. The Dutch speak the units first and the tens second; even if they speak English well, this may lead to some confusion. For instance, 98,000 spoken by your Dutch counterpart could mean 89,000 to your partner. Check in writing before concluding the deal.

Do not be late for the meeting, and use your business card; this is very important to the Dutch. Small talk is acceptable in the meeting. The Dutch are proud of their houses, offices and cars and these are personally important to them. In your presentations, do not understate your case or achievements (a British phenomenon!); the Dutch will view this either as a lack of commitment or take it literally. At all times, be direct and honest in your business affairs. The Dutch will be good partners except when you don't deliver. No delivery is the supplier's fault, regardless of the reason. The Dutch are more likely to stop doing business with you for not fulfilling a delivery date (within reason) than to sue you.

The Dutch are very good negotiators and can be a trifle ruthless. They tend not to be particularly nationalistic, but it does pay to introduce yourself in Dutch, to have some knowledge of the Dutch Royal Family and ministers, and to understand something of the Dutch culture. It is also important to avoid calling their country Holland, which in fact refers only to a couple of the provinces and not to the whole of the country.

ENTERTAINING

Business meals

Lunch in the Netherlands is taken fairly early; between 12.30 pm and 1.30 pm. If you are not invited do not take this as a slight, it is not a negative reaction; to be invited is a positive indicator in your favour. The Dutch hate pretension (and remember their thriftiness!), so lunch is unlikely to be elaborate; more likely a beer and a sandwich. Whoever issues the invitation, pays the bill.

Breakfast meetings are not common, but dinner is a more relaxed affair. Business is generally not conducted over dinner. Formal entertainment of the 'sponsorship' type is not common in the Netherlands, but informal arrangements are.

If you are invited to your host's home, do not take wine: flowers or chocolate for the hostess are expected. Because of the Netherland's flower industry, you should spend approximately £8 to £10 on flowers for the 'right' sized bunch. Greetings are formal; handshaking is important and, when meeting the hostess, should be offered. More familiar associates will kiss cheek-to-cheek; do not do it, wait for the hostess to offer. A letter of thanks for hospitality is always welcome, as is the offer of reciprocal entertainment in your home.

Subjects for social discussion

The Dutch are well informed on British news. They are major trading partners with the UK, with nearly 15 per cent of their exports going into Britain. Because they receive BBC television, they are as up-to-date as most Britons on British current affairs. The restricted use of their language internationally requires that they maintain a wide European perspective. The Dutch enjoy their business success and are usually happy to discuss business-related topics. Sport, especially football, Dutch culture and family life are safe subjects. The Dutch sense of humour is very similar to the British.

Business hospitality

The Dutch are not exhibitionists, and thus business hospitality is unlikely to include lavish corporate events. Personal invitations are given more out of genuine personal friendship than out of corporate ambition.

Gifts

Only business-type brand gifts are usual. These should not be ostentatious, and certainly will not help in shaping the business deal.

Dress

Well-dressed and semi-formal is the key to business dressing in the Netherlands. Blazer and slacks are acceptable for men, although suits are safest, with smart ties and shirts. Ties are retained at all times. Women have greater flexibility, but should always remain smart.

WOMEN IN BUSINESS

Women have open access to business, but still form a small percentage of senior managers.

WORKING HOURS AND PUBLIC HOLIDAYS

The core working time in the Netherlands is 9.00 am to 5.30 pm, but younger executives will usually add an hour on either side of these times. After work, they are likely to go straight home but will, unlike the Germans, expect to take work home with them. Telephone calls outside office hours will be welcomed, provided there is a real urgency about the business message.

On average, the Dutch have four weeks' holiday a year, which is split into two holidays: a winter sports, and a longer summer holiday. The summer season, between mid-July to mid-August is to be avoided.

1st January	(New Year's Day)
30th April	(Queen's Birthday)
25th/26th December	(Christmas Day)

In addition, there are four movable days, including Good Friday and Easter Monday.

LETTER-WRITING

The envelope

Dutch	English
De Heer (initials, surname)	Mr
Mevrouw (initials, surname)	Mrs
Mejuffrouw (initials, surname)	Miss

Salutation

Letter written in:	
Dutch	English
Geachte Heer (surname)	Dear Mr (surname)
Geachte Mevrouw (surname)	Dear Mrs (surname)
Geachte Mejuffrouw (surname)	Dear Miss (surname)
Geachte Heer/Geachte Mevrouw	Dear Sir, Dear Madam
Mijne Heren	Dear Sirs

Closing

Individual	Hoogachtend (or less formally) met vriendelÿke groeten hoogachtend	Yours sincerely
Company	Hoogachtend	Yours faithfully

Note

Initials only are used, not forenames. Letters (eg for professional qualifications) are used after the surname, but only on the envelope. A person's business card is generally a good indicator of how he likes to be addressed. Except at senior level, it is usual to write to the department concerned and not to the individual.

MARKETING

Advertising expenditure has a higher growth rate than GNP with 8.4 per cent growth in 1986 over 1985. The most significant element in the budget, compared with other countries, is direct advertising which, together with sales promotion, sponsorship and public relations, claims up to two-thirds of the advertising expenditure.

Satellite and cable television are matched by three Dutch television channels, forging a sophisticated board and narrow-cost media framework. New magazines and the re-emergence of posters complete the picture.

Consumers are classified in a similar manner to the UK, but with classification 'B' split, rather than 'C'.

Table 14.2   Consumer classification in percentage of population in the Netherlands

Socio-economic class	%
A	16
B_1/B_2	29
C	39
D	16

Source   Summo Scanner, 1987

The media DFL is divided in the following way:

Table 14.3   Media spend in the Netherlands

	%
Newspapers	34
Magazines	11
TV	5
Skychannel	1
Radio	1
Outdoors (including sports sponsorship)	4
Direct advertising	44

Source   VEA

The spend rankings by key categories are:

Table 14.4   Key categories spend ranking in the Netherlands

(1)	Banks, insurance, finance
(2)	Cars, motorcycles
(3)	Food
(4)	Travel
(5)	Alcoholic drinks
(6)	Radios, TVs, record players
(7)	Household cleaners
(8)	Tobacco

Source   Bureau voor Budgellen Controle (BBC)

Media

There is no specific advertising tax. VAT is levied at 20 per cent on all media with the exception of press media published four or more times a year, for which the rate is 6 per cent. Certain restrictions are placed on advertisements for tobacco and cigarettes, alcoholic drinks, medicinal products and treatments, direct marketing, consumer credit loans, investment, property and sweets. No tobacco products may be advertised on TV. As from 1 January 1988, responsibility for compiling and supervising the rules and regulations on advertising in all media, including radio and TV, now rests with *De Stichting Reclame Code*. Westermarkt 2, 1016 DK Amsterdam (Tel: (+31) 20 257690/257721).

There are 49 daily titles, with a total daily circulation of 4.5 million copies and an average reach of 8.1 million persons (aged fifteen and over). Many of the leading dailies have local editions, and some publish colour supplements. The newspaper market, as far as dailies are concerned, is currently stable. Of the non-dailies (which include weeklies and papers published twice and three times a week) 129 belong to the *Nederslandse Nieuwsblad Pers*, which does not account for all non-dailies in existence. Over 700 free-sheets are published, with a total estimated circulation of six million copies. There are no Sunday papers in the Netherlands. The country offers a wide selection of magazines; however, not all of these carry advertising.

CONSUMER PREFERENCES/DIFFERENCES

Household spend

The Dutch have a lot in common with their Northern European neighbours, spending a high proportion of their money on furniture for the home. The same applies to household equipment, for example, more fridges are sold in the Netherlands than in any other member state.

Interestingly, the Dutch consumer, unlike the Italians or French, does not rank his first purchase consideration to be a home produced product. Quality and price are foremost considerations.

The breakdown of household spend on goods and services is as follows.

Table 14.5   Household spend in the Netherlands

Items	%
Furniture (including carpets and other floor coverings)	40
White goods	12
Furnishings	8
Table utensils	14
Domestic and other household services	26

Source   Eurostat/Mintel

Financial awareness

Although they have the second largest options exchange in the world based in Amsterdam, the Dutch do not follow the Northern European trend of being financially aware. Fewer bank accounts are held in the Netherlands than in any other Northern European country. Their personal financial profile is more similar to that found in Mediterranean countries. This trend could change after 1992.

Food spend

Unlike their neighbours in Germany, the Dutch food spend is concentrated more on fresh produce than on tinned or frozen items. Beer and wine is consumed but not in any great volume.

The Dutch drink a considerable volume of coffee, second only to the Germans.

General consumer spend

The Dutch have one of the lowest rates of motorcycle owner-ship in the Community but the highest ownership of stereos.

As mentioned previously, they have little preference for pur-chasing durables, cars etc made in their own country. Given an increase in their spending power they would prefer a meal out than doing DIY!

Political trends

The Christian Democrats Party still retains popular support throughout the Netherlands, holding two-fifths of the Netherland's Euro seats.

However, voter awareness of the Euro elections is well below that of its neighbours, showing a 47 per cent turnout.

Green issues are still presented by the Rainbow Party: the number of seats won in 1989 remained at two, showing that Green issues were holding.

ESTABLISHING A BUSINESS

The position of a foreign-owned company in the Netherlands is essentially the same as that of a Dutch-owned company. All new entities must comply with registration rules and meet vari-ous environmental and business requirements.

Every new business must be registered with the Trade Regi-ster of the Chamber of Commerce in the area in which it is located. Appointments of trade agents who have full powers of attorney to deal on behalf of foreign principals must also be reg-istered.

The information to be filed in the register includes:

1. A copy of the articles of incorporation of the enterprise, including its name, its trade name, if different, its objectives and its registered address.
2. The amounts of authorised, issued and paid-in capital, and the names and addresses of any shareholders who have not fully paid in the capital contributions on their shares.
3. The names and personal particulars of the supervisory and managing directors.
4. The powers of each managing director.

Other requirements, including permits and formalities to be dealt with, are those arising from:

1. The Public Nuisance Act: this Act requires a licence to be

obtained from the municipal authorities if any dangerous or disagreeable trade is to be carried on.

2. The Pollution of Surface Waters Act and the Air Pollution Act.
3. Other laws such as building regulations, the Factories Act, and the Shops Act.

Every new enterprise must also register with the office of direct taxation, indirect taxation (the VAT inspectorate) and social security.

An existing enterprise that already possesses all the necessary permits and licences, but is then acquired by foreigners, does not need to renew those permits and licences.

There are no requirements for Dutch participation in either the equity captial of a business entity or in its management. There are two types of limited liability company: the smaller *Besloten Vennootschap (BV)* private company, and the larger *Naamloze Vennootschap (NV)*. The legal requirements are very similar, but they differ in capitalisation and the nature of shares.

The minimum capital for a BV is DF 40,000 and for a NV DF 100,000. The BV can only have registered shares and cannot issue share certificates, whereas the NV can issue registered or bearer shares.

Management structure

Every company must have a managing director, or a management board with any appropriate number of members. In addition, a large company must have a supervisory board, consisting of at least three individuals. A 'large company' for this purpose is one:

1. with issued capital and consolidated reserves of DF 22.5 million or more;
2. which has established a works council (either itself or in a subsidiary company);
3. which, together with its subsidiary companies (if any), has 100 or more employees in the Netherlands.

The same rules apply to BV and NV companies.

In a large company (whether BV or NV), the supervisory board is solely resposible for appointing and dismissing the members of the management board, finalising the annual financial statements, and approving a number of major management decisions.

Shareholders, works councils and the management board itself are, however, entitled to nominate candidates for the supervisory board; the first two of these groups have a limited right of veto over proposed appointments by the supervisory board, although this right is exercised only in very exceptional circumstances.

In subsidiaries of foreign parent companies, even if these subsidiaries qualify as large companies, the authority to appoint and dismiss members of the management board and to finalise the annual financial statements may under certain conditions be reserved for the shareholders.

A smaller company may also institute a supervisory board in certain circumstances if it so decides, setting out the board's powers and duties in its articles of incorporation. Normally in such a case, the members of both boards are appointed and dismissed by the shareholders. Supervisory board members are not allowed to be executives or employees of the company; their function is to advise and supervise the company's management.

Every company with 100 or more employees who work more than one-third of normal working hours, must set up a works council made up by its employees. This council must be given, on demand, all the information it needs to perform its duties. In general, the council must be consulted on matters such as mergers, the set-up or closure of a business and important changes in the company's organisation, and must give its consent to proposals on employment policies, the hiring and training of personnel, safety regulations, etc. In companies with less than 100 employees, works councils' rights are slightly reduced.

Employees have no legal rights to elect members directly to either the supervisory or the management board. The works council must, however, be consulted on proposed nominations to the management board. Moreover, in large companies (as already defined) the works council is entitled to propose candidates for the supervisory board and object to nominations to that board.

Companies with 10–34 employees must enable the labour force to debate twice-yearly with the management board all important matters concerning the company.

SINGLE-MARKET EFFORTS

Government

A conference was held on 26 November 1988 to enhance awareness of 1992. A campaign was launched in September of that year and included a 'Euroline' telephone hotline. Information packs have been distributed to businessmen and a database has been set up. A 'Euro Bulletin' (ten editions each year) has also been launched to provide continuous updates on progress in the Single Market.

Surveys

The Economic Affairs Ministry survey was released in September 1988 and showed a 71 per cent awareness of the Single Market. Of this 55 per cent were aware of specific proposals relevant to their business, but only 42 per cent expected completion of the Single Market by 1992.

USEFUL ADDRESSES

Sources of information and help

Netherlands-British Chamber of Commerce
The Dutch House
307-308 High Holborn
London WC1V 7LS
Tel: 01-405 1538

Netherlands-British Chamber of Commerce
Holland Trade House
Bezuidenhoutseweg 181
2594 AH
The Hague
Tel: (31) 70 47 8881
Tlx: 33122

Research sources

A.C. Nielsen Company
Amsteldijk 166
1079 LH
Amsterdam
Tel: (+31) 20 444972
Tlx: 112659

Orange Nassaulaan 25 (qualitative research specialists)
P O Box 1075
AJ Amsterdam
Tel: (+31) 20 750071

Addresses for advertisers

Nederlandse Verenigning van Erkende Reclame-Adviesbureax
(advertising agency)
A J Ernstraat 169
Amsterdam
Tel: (+31) 20 425642

Veldkamp Marktonderzoet (social science surveys/market analysis)
Stadhouderskade 159
1074 BC
Amsterdam
Tel: (+31) 20 731125

Chamber of Commerce

Amsterdam   Koningin Wilhelminaplein 13
             Amsterdam
             Tel: (+31) 20 172882

The Hague   Alexander Gogelweg 16
             The Hague
             Tel: (+31) 70 614101

Rotterdam   Coolsingel 58
             Rotterdam
             Tel: (+31) 10 145022

Principal Euro Info Centres

EG-Adviescentrum voor Ondernemigen
9 Dalstandreef/BP 112
NL-1112 XC Dremen-Zuid
Tel: (+31) 20 90 10 71

EG-Adviescentrum voor Ondernemigen
Prins Henenklaan Zlu
Postbus 955
NL-5700 AZ Helmond
Tel: (+31) 49 20 48 468

15
PORTUGAL

INTRODUCTION

The Portuguese, although inhabitants of part of the same penin-
sula as Spain, are quite a different nation from the Spanish.
They maintain the Mediterranean pride of the Spanish, but
couple it more with humanity than arrogance. It is worth
remembering that, like the Dutch, the Portuguese were a strong
trading nation and as such have close ties with some European
partners. Although outsiders may couple the Spanish and Portuguese together in their minds, the Anglo-Portuguese relationship, for example, is longer in duration than any trading
similarities there may be between the two Iberian nations.

Portugal is the poorest country in the Community. The economic facts have done nothing to dampen the Portuguese's
pride in their past or the hospitality and downright friendliness
of the people.

Their most recent history is dominated by the 1974 revolution,
which is of similar sensitivity in discussion as Franco's Spain.
Power, although now spread more equally owing to democracy,
is, in business, still vested in 13 core families.

The country has no traditional North/South divide; there are
the tourist centres of the Algarve, and then there is the rest of
the country. There are two major business centres: Lisbon, and
the more industrial Oporto.

Generally, the Portuguese expect much to come from their
membership of the Community; they understand Portugal's
lower production costs and wish to exploit them. The country's
infrastructure is still struggling to match the revolutionary
awakening of the country and, although education is valued, it
is given by the state in two shifts: 8.00 am–12.30 pm, and 1.30–
6.00 pm. The rich still retain a grip on the economy of the country, through their domination of the better private education system.

MAKING THE APPOINTMENT

A personal introduction is probably the best way of beginning a business relationship. If this is not possible, however, a letter is the next best approach. It can be in your own language; the Portuguese will not be offended by you not using their language, although they will be pleased if you do. The offer of an interpreter will also be welcomed. However, the likelihood of a written response is low. A telephone call within a week of your expected interview to confirm it would be wise.

The letter and telephone call should be directed to the head of the company, who will be willing and able to talk to you directly. The need to be protected from outsiders is of little interest to the Portuguese; the role of the secretary, therefore, is less significant than, say, in the UK. She is more likely to be a typist and message-taker.

THE MEETING

You should arrive on time for the meeting, but do be prepared to wait – two hours is not unusual. It is a brave person, however, who is willing to gamble and arrive late for a meeting with the Portuguese. Once the meeting is under way, discussion will be friendly and probably protracted, although the tone of the meeting will still remain quite formal after the initial hand-shaking. However, you will probably not get down to business straight away, so be prepared for some small talk and take the lead from your host. (Football and the beauty of Portugal are useful topics of conversation.)

Unlike most European countries, the qualification of a first degree also allows the use of the title 'Doctor'. You need to recognise that this title does not have the implications which pertain to it in other countries, but it is still polite to use it where appropriate.

The discussion will naturally lead to a business meal, where the final deal may be agreed. The Portuguese will agree in principle to the deal and then bring in their lawyers to finalise it. The deal will be honoured very much in the French style. The Portuguese tend to find it difficult to understand the importance of delivery dates. They will be hard to pin down, and surprised at the concern you show at a few days' or weeks' delay. Be prepared for a strong insistence on price; almost everything else is negotiable except the price to be paid. They will walk away from a deal rather than negotiate. In general, the Portuguese view the British as by far the most effective and efficient nation in the Community.

ENTERTAINING

Business meals

The Portuguese business day is weighted towards the evening. Breakfast meetings are unusual, but may be taken at nine or ten o'clock. Lunch is much more likely to be taken as a business extension. They will not drink excessively at lunch; one or two bottles of wine is usual, but they will not be offended if you do not drink or try to keep up. Lunch is likely to last for about two hours.

Dinner is also seen as an extension of the business day and an invitation to dinner, normally taken away from the home, is of no great significance (nor, in fact, is having dinner at your counterpart's home). If dinner is taken out, it is unlikely that your counterpart's wife will be invited. You should not press for this, even if you have dined at his home on previous occasions.

Take care to compliment the food, as this is very important to the Portuguese. Do not be surprised at the frequency of their smoking, and do not order Mateus Rosé. If you have extended the invitation, then you may offer to pay the bill but you should not insist as it is unlikely that you will succeed.

If you are entertained at home, flowers and chocolates are acceptable gifts, but make sure that red carnations are not included in any bouquet (they are the emblem of the revolution).

As a foreigner, you will find the hospitality extremely generous. It is quite possible, after only a short business relationship, to be invited away for the weekend with the family to their holiday home. A note of gratitude is well received, and should be sent within a couple of days of the trip. There is little in the way of formal business 'sponsorship' entertaining.

Subjects for social discussion

In general discussion, sport, the family and home are important, cars less so. Cultural history is also very important and images of the Portuguese equivalent of Shakespeare, Luis de Camoes, are currently used in many product promotions.

Business hospitality

It is very unlikely that corporate entertainment facilities will be available or offered, except by the major multinational companies. In general, business hospitality is conducted at a very personal level.

Gifts

Business gifts are restricted to small, acceptable items, perhaps with the company logo. The issue of 'generous' gifts to those who helped secure business is much less common today than in the past, although misappropriation of funds is not unknown.

Dress

Smart but informal dress is acceptable, although at the initial business meeting it would be prudent to stick to the conservative, lightweight business suit. Women should wear classic, feminine styles.

WOMEN IN BUSINESS

Few women are found in business in Portugal. Women tend to be regarded very much as wives and mothers first. The growth in education is helping to develop a better role for women in business, but, as in Greece, attitudes are changing very slowly.

WORKING HOURS AND PUBLIC HOLIDAYS

The normal office hours are 9.00 am–5.00 pm in Lisbon; in Oporto, factories will start an hour earlier. Out of office meetings will begin any time after 7.00 pm. It is not unusual for any of the professions to be working until midnight (an 11.30 dental appointment could well be in the evening). Business calls at home up until that time are the norm, and you should expect to receive them yourself. August is the month when most holidays are taken, and it is very difficult to do business during that time.

Public holidays are:

1st January	(New Year's Day)
25th April	(National Day)
1st May	(Labour Day)
10th June	(Camoes' Day)
13th June	(St Anthony's Day [Lisbon])
24th June	(St John's Day [Oporto])
15th August	(Assumption)
5th October	(Republic Day)
1st November	(All Saints' Day)
1st December	(Restoration Day)
8th December	(Immaculate Conception)
25th December	(Christmas Day)

There are, in addition, two movable days, including Good Friday.

LETTER-WRITING

The envelope

Portuguese	English
Exmº Senhor (forenames, surname)	Mr
Exmª Senhora D. (forenames, surname)	Mrs
Not used in business letters	Miss

Salutation

| | Letter written in: |
Portuguese	English
Exmªᵈ Senhor (forenames, surname)	Dear Mr (surname) or Dear Senhor (surname)
Exmª Senhora D. (surname)	Dear Mrs (surname) or Dear Senhora D. (surname)
Exmº Senhor, Exmª Senhora	Dear Sir, Dear Madam
Exmºs Senhores	Dear Sirs

Closing
Individual
Com os melhores cumprimentos, subscrevemo-me	Yours sincerely
De V. Exª	
Atentamente	

Company
Com os melhores cumprimentos, subscrevemo-nos,	Yours faithfully
De V. Exª	
Atentamente	

When sending a letter bear in mind the following points:

• Always use full forenames rather than initials on the envelope, and in the salutation, unless there are more than four.

- A wife can choose whether or not to take her husband's surname. If so, it is added to her existing family name. Men have just their family name.
- In business, address Miss as Mrs.
- If writing to a person one knows, it is usual to substitute 'Caro' for Exm° Senhor, followed by the forenames and surname.

MARKETING

The advertising market in Portugal is booming. This is due to a growth in business through Portugal's membership of the European Community. This has lead to big, international accounts being lined up with international agencies, and so these agencies are becoming more important than local agencies. The growth rate in advertising spending of 1987 over 1986 was 50 per cent. Although this has now slowed down a little, it gives some idea of the potential.

The country's consumers have been classified in a similar way to the UK, and are weighted in the following way:

Table 15.1   Consumer classification in Portugal

	%
AB	5
C_1	31
C_2	57
D	7

Source   Quantum, Lisbon

The advertising escudo is spent in the following media:

Table 15.2   Media spend in Portugal

	%
Press	26
TV	54
Radio	13
Cinema	2
Outdoor	5

Source   Sabatina

The spend rankings by key categories are:

Table 15.3   Key categories spend in Portugal

(1) Food
(2) Alcoholic beverages
(3) Other beverages
(4) Automotive
(5) Publishing
(6) Lotteries

Source   Sabatina

Media

VAT is charged at 16 per cent. Taxes are liable on advertisements placed on TV at a rate of 2 per cent, radio at 3 per cent,
cinema at 2 per cent, daily newspapers at 1 per cent while all
other print media are liable to a 16 per cent advertisement tax.
On outdoor advertising there is a levy of Esc 20 per square metre
per month, with a discount on bookings of 10 square metres and
above. No tobacco advertising is allowed except on outdoor
media for a six-month period following the launch of a new
brand. Alcoholic drinks may be advertised on TV and radio after
10.00 pm, but the advertisement may not show a person drinking. There are no restrictions on alcohol advertisement, in print
or outdoor. All pharmaceutical product advertising must be
approved by the relevant health authority. For further information contact: Portuguese Association of Advertising Agencies,
Rua Rodrigo da Fonseca, 20–4, 4–DTO, 1000 Lisbon (Tel: (+351)
1 656518).

CONSUMER PREFERENCES/DIFFERENCES

Few statistics are available on the consumer habits in Portugal.
What does emerge is noted below.

Household spend

In Portugal, there are low levels of ownership in electric appliances, this is not only true on the household appliance level but
also for personal computers etc. However, per capita, Portugal
has more stoves than its Iberian neighbour. As Portugal's
wealth increases so will her demand for consumer/household
items.

This is not to say that the statistics indicate that the Portuguese spend very little on their homes. They do spend on their homes but because of the low level of income they remain at the bottom of the consumer spend table.

Financial awareness

Although most international banks have a presence in Lisbon and the major tourist centres, the use of banks and other financial institutions is limited. The same applies for credit cards.

Food spend

The Portuguese eat more poultry than any other meat; however, they have the lowest *per capita* spend on meat in the Community.

General consumer spend

The Portuguese are at the bottom of the EC league spend table when it comes to dressing themselves. Indeed, on average, the men spend more on their beer and wine than on their clothes. This is despite having a growing clothes manufacturing industry.

Political trends

The Socialist Party gained one seat although they were still in second place to the Christian Democrats. Out of a total of 24 Euro seats, 51 per cent of Portuguese voters turned out to elect their representatives.

ESTABLISHING A BUSINESS

Every new enterprise must register with the Commercial Register and the tax division of the Ministry of Finance. Most businesses are required to join an employers' guild and pay an annual fee to cover guild expenses. All investments must comply with health, security and environmental protection regulations. Investors planning large development projects are required to prepare a report on the likely ecological impact, for approval by the State Secretary for the Environment, before operations may commence. Industrial buildings must conform to standards established by the Ministry of Industry for the relevant sector, for example, concerning the distance between buildings.

The Portuguese legislation was rationalised in the 1986 Code, which incorporated the various and appropriate EC directives. This provided for four types of company formation:

1. The private limited liability or 'quota' company: *Sociedades por Quotas de Responsabilidade Limitada (Lda)*.
2. The corporation: *Sociedade Anonima de Responsabilidade Limitada (SA)*.

3. A partnership: *Sociedade en Nome Colectivo (SNC)*.
4. Two types of limited partnership.

The Lda is usually for smaller companies where the public capital is not required. An SA, however, is more complex, allowing the attraction of public money on the Stock Exchange.

An Lda minimum capitalisation is Esc 400,000, and each quota must have a minimum value of Esc 250. The minimum capital required for *Sociedade Anomina* is Esc 5,000,000, represented by shares with par value of no less than Esc 1,000.

Management structure

The management structure of an SA can be two- or three-tier. The two-tier structure has a Board of Directors (*Conselho de Administraçao*) and a Board of Auditors (*Conselho Fiscal*), whilst the three-tier consists of a directorate *(Direcçao)*, the general board (*Conselho Geral*) and a statutory auditor (*Revisor Oficial de Contas*). Both structures have to be agreed in advance. The three-tier structure is the more modern.

In the traditional two-tier company, the Board of Directors undertakes the general management and the Board of Auditors has the role of supervising the company. Direct representation from the shareholders sit on the Board of Auditors. In the newer, three-tier form, the Directorate is composed of an uneven number of no more than five directors. The directors are normally appointed by the General Council. The Council cannot consist of more than 15 people, elected at a general shareholders' meeting, and its duties include electing and removing the directors, reviewing the supervisory actions of the directorate and verifying the corporation financial statements. Finally, there is the Statutory Auditor who must be a shareholder and who is appointed to examine the company accounts.

A 'quota' company is managed by one or more managers appointed by the members. A manager need not be a Portuguese national or resident. A member of the company may become a manager. A quota company, unlike an SA, is not required by law to have a Board of Auditors.

The law does not require workers' representatives to be included on the board of managers. However, workers' committees with three to eleven members, depending on the size of the company concerned, must be established. These committees must be given information, including financial information, but may not participate in corporate management.

SINGLE-MARKET EFFORTS

Government

A 1992 Office is being established which will be responsible for running an awareness campaign beginning in spring 1989. A Single Market public telephone line opened on 9 May 1989. A basic information pack on the Single Market was released in October 1988. The Industry Ministry is advertising the PEDIP programme (a Community fund for modernising Portuguese industry) and linking this with the Single Market; 1992 continues to be a major theme of ministerial speeches.

Business

There are a large number of business seminars, notably those organised by Portuguese Industry Association, Industry Association of Oporto (industrial centre) and the Portuguese Banking Federation. An EC information office has been established in Oporto as a joint project between the Industry Association of Oporto and the Commission.

Surveys

There have been no recent surveys. Awareness of 1992 is widespread, but there is little realistion of the actual implications for Portugal.

USEFUL ADDRESSES

Sources of information and help

Portuguese Chamber of Commerce and Industry in the UK
4th Floor
New Bond Street House
1–5 New Bond Street
London W1Y 9PE
Tel: 01-493 9973

British–Portuguese Chamber of Commerce
Rua da Estrella 8
P-1200 Lisbon
Tel: (+351) 1 661586
Tlx: 12787 BRICHA P

Research sources

A.C. Nielsen Company (continuous retail audits)
Rua Rosa Aranjo 34.4

P-1200 Lisbon
Tel: (+351) 1 554412
Tlx: 12748

Addresses for advertisers
Portuguese Association of Advertising Agencies
Rua Rodrigo da Fonseca 20–4
4-DTO
1000 Lisbon
Tel: (+351) 1 656518

Chambers of Commerce
Lisbon   Rua de Santo Antao 88
Lisbon
Tel: (+351) 1 327289

Oporto   Palacio da Bolsa
Oporto
Tel: (+351) 2 24497

Principal Euro Info Centres
Eurogabinete
Exponur
Leca de Palmeira
P-4450 Matosinhos
Tel: (+351) 29 956940

Eurogabinete
Av Casbal Ribeiro 59
P-1000 Lisbon
Tel: (+351) 1 561071

16
SPAIN

INTRODUCTION

Like most of the Community countries, Spain has regional
dissimilarities, but they are perhaps the most pronounced and
wide-ranging of all the countries within the EC. To treat Spain
as one country would be a bad mistake. The Catalonians, the
Basques, and the Andalusians are quite different people, with
different subcultures and business styles.

For instance, a typical Andalusian will be difficult to do business with, unsure of the honesty of his trading partner. He will
counter question with question. The Basque and the Andalusian
belief in independence will extend to gifts being freely given to
ensure that no debt is being incurred by the deal. In Catalonia,
however, the people are more European in attitude and outlook.
In all cases, the generation gap plays a major role; younger
executives are more able to focus on business deals, although
contacting the correct person within this group is more important – and more difficult – in order to reduce internal political
problems than it is with the older, mainly non-English-speaking
generation.

In general, it is true to say that the Spaniards are a proud,
even haughty, nation giving to perceiving slights where none
are intended, but this is balanced by their generosity and socia-
bility, which are difficult to match elsewhere.

MAKING THE APPOINTMENT

It is important to contact the Spanish executive with whom you
wish to do business. This should be done in a well-written, formal letter. A telephone call within two weeks of sending the letter is acceptable. However, be sure that the contact is correct;
not only is the Spanish business hierarchy very formal (and prepared, in some cases, to accept 'gifts'), there is also considerable
jealousy of success. A commitment made by one executive can

and might be overturned by his senior if he perceives it as being outside the other's range of business.

Spanish business executives also work very hard at making relationships which are hard to break, regardless of the quality of the new sales proposition. If you suspect that a deal will not progress on its merits, then a telephone call to the Managing Director may break the logjam. This, must be done with great skill so as not to create loss of face for the executive who is subsequently instructed to respond to your initiative.

The role of the secretary is growing. In major companies she plays a very European role in handling the executive's diary. The secretary is seen very much as the 'office wife', to look after the business needs of the executive. If treated in this way, with courtesy, she will be very valuable. However, given the social structure of Spain, she will always remain an 'assistant-to', and will be unlikely to undertake agreements, even to arrange meetings, without further confirmation.

In all communications, especially in open transmission such as telex and facsimile, ensure the sensitivity of the issue is recognised. If you upset a Spanish executive by allowing others to read or react to your requests more effectively than your counterpart is able, it could lead to a deal which might have been done (slowly, perhaps – but done) being stopped. The biggest single problem in doing business is inside politics and envy.

THE MEETING

If you are attending a meeting and are unable to speak Spanish, enquire first of your counterpart if he wishes to discuss business in English, or has someone on his staff who could act as interpreter. Only as the last option offer to bring your own interpreter.

The Spanish, particularly in Southern Spain, are passionate about their business and express themselves in a great deal of non-verbal behaviour – don't, however, take the lead in this. Back-slapping and hugging is initiated by the Spanish in all but the most intimate and long-standing relationships.

Spanish business meetings can go on for a long time and, if lunch or dinner is offered, even longer. In the small talk surrounding the business propositions the subjects of football and bullfighting (if positive) are acceptable. However, politics is not. Never join in or show a preference for one side or the other; the Franco days cut deeply into many families.

During the meeting, try to avoid a lecturing approach. The Spanish like to take their time and be seen to be in control of the discussion. To force them to an 'obvious' conclusion will be self-defeating. The greatest emphases will be placed on a good personal relationship and trust. Any contract entered into will be strictly fulfilled, and they will expect no less of you. The passion which is so typically Mediterranean will be used during negotiations and, unless you back them into an impossible position, will be temporary. Haggling is an accepted tactic, and its use is expected. Once an agreement is made, the terms and the spirit will be honored in the fullest sense, even if personal loss is its consequence. If this is caused by an error by both parties to the deal, the approach must be handled carefully to avoid loss of face.

ENTERTAINING

Business meals

Business lunches take hours, and are usually lavish and alcoholic. The Spanish are used to this, but the large quantities of alcohol may put you at a disadvantage. Lunch begins at about 1.30–2.00 pm with drinks, and can finish around 4.30–5.00 pm. The Spanish will expect you to join and match him in the consumption of drinks; not to do so without an adequate excuse is seen as unfriendly, and medical excuses are the best accepted. Business and non-business topics will be discussed throughout the meal, so you need to remain sharp throughout.

Breakfast meetings are acceptable, but need to be checked out before being offered. Dinner, if taken out, will be between 10.00–11.00 pm.

Being taken to someone's home is a great sign of trust. If you are invited to join your counterpart and his family this is very positive, although it does vary from province to province and is less likely to occur, for example, in Catalonia, where business and pleasure are very separate. For dinner, you are likely to be invited at 8.30 pm for drinks with the meal being served around 9.30 pm. Spanish hospitality and generosity are a way of life. A Spaniard – even if he has little money – will want to pay for the meal regardless of who extends the invitation. It is always polite to offer, but accept that you are unlikely to end up paying.

Subjects for social discussion

It is important to comment upon the family, and children in particular. The Spanish in general enjoy children, and take great pride in their families. If you have a family yourself, this can help. Other areas of discussion are cultural, but remember that there are provincial rivalries so make sure your compliments are appropriate to the region.

Business hospitality

Business hospitality is unusual in Spain, although invitations in the major cultural centres may be offered. In general, the Spanish would expect you to perceive their generous personal hospitality as more important than corporate entertainment.

Gifts

In Spain, it is not the custom to take gifts for the host or hostess when being entertained at a person's home. *Never* take any. It is acceptable, however, when leaving the country, to send flowers to the lady of the house, thanking her for her hospitality. When you are introduced to the hostess, do not introduce yourself by kissing cheeks. Wait for her to offer hers. Business associates are expected to act according to their perceived cultures, and the British and Dutch are considered to be somewhat distant.

Business gifts, however, are an accepted part of Spanish business life. They are used to cement continuing relationships. Christmas presents in Spain can be very expensive. However, there is a growing backlash against this type of present. Find out the culture within the particular company with whom you are dealing: to get it wrong either way could damage both the personal and business relationship.

Dress

A dark-coloured suit and conservative tie are an important part of dress-sense in Spain, although in the provinces a blazer or sports jacket with slacks is acceptable. It is important to look both serious and stylish.

WOMEN IN BUSINESS

Women are not expected to (and therefore usually do not) reach senior levels of management. Men, although polite, are unlikely to treat a woman with the same peer-level respect as a male counterpart would command. Business with a woman may well take longer and be culturally more difficult for a Spaniard (particularly of the older generation) to deal with.

WORKING HOURS AND PUBLIC HOLIDAYS

The day is divided into two. An 8.30 or 9.00 am start is usual with work continuing until 1.00 pm. Lunch, particularly in the provinces, is usually taken at home and never in the office which closes until 4.30 pm. Work then recommences until about 7.30–8.30 pm. In summertime, this changes and the offices are only open from 7.30 am until 2.30 pm. This is called *journada intensive*. Those offices which need to remain open will only have a skeleton staff.

Public holidays are:

1st January	(New Year's Day)
6th January	(Epiphany)
19th March	(St Joseph's Day)
1st May	(Labour Day)
25th July	(St James's Day)
15th August	(Assumption)
12th October	(Columbus' Day)
1st November	(All Saints' Day)
8th December	(Immaculate Conception)
25th December	(Christmas Day)

In addition, there are three movable days, including Good Friday and Easter Monday.

LETTER-WRITING

The envelope

Spanish	English
Sr D (initials, surnames)	Mr
Sra Doña (initials, surnames)	Mrs
Srta (initials surnames)	Miss

Salutation

Spanish	Letter written in: English
Muy Sr mío	Dear Mr (first surname)
	Dear Sr (first surname)
Muy Sra mía	Dear Mrs (first surname)
	Dear Sra (first surname)
Srta (first surname)	Dear Miss (first surname)
	Dear Srta (first surname)
Muy Sr mío, Muy Sra mía	Dear Sir, Madam
Muy Srs míos	Dear Sirs

Closing

Individual	Le saluda atentamente	Yours sincerely
Company	Le saluda atentamente	Yours faithfully

Note
If the letter is written in Spanish, the surname is omitted in the salutation.

MARKETING

Advertising expenditure has grown by 25 per cent per annum since 1984. This increase in expenditure had benefited all segments of the media alike, with media owners launching competitive media to provide a full range of services. Research facilities to match the greater range of media opportunities are also rapidly being developed in a country whose 40 million inhabitants are seen as a core attraction by many EC countries.

The consumer base has five classifications and is broken down as follows:

Table 16.1   Consumer classifications in Spain

	%
Upper	7.0
Upper Middle	20.0
Middle	32.0
Lower Middle	18.0
Lower	23.0

Source   INE

Spending is split in the media as follows:

Table 16.2   Media spend in Spain

	%
Newspapers	33.0
Magazines	17.0
Television	32.0
Radio	13.0
Cinema	0.5
Outdoor	4.5

Source   JWT, Madrid

The spend rankings by key categories are:

Table 16.3   *Key categories spend in Spain*

(1)   Food
(2)   Transport (including cars)
(3)   Alcoholic and non-alcoholic drinks
(4)   Beauty and hygiene
(5)   Services, public and private
(6)   Finance, insurance
(7)   Commerce
(8)   Household goods
(9)   Tobacco

Source   Repress (Nielsen)

Media

All advertising in Spain, except in the Canary Islands, is subject to VAT (known as TVA) at 12 per cent. Television advertising of alcoholic drinks, tobacco and prescription drugs is prohibited in all parts of Spain. Advertisements for financial and pharmaceutical products require administrative authorisation.

CONSUMER PREFERENCES/DIFFERENCES

Household spend

The Spanish desire a beautiful home above most things and this is reflected on the amount they spend on the furnishings for their home. Because they have a strong home market, however, furnishings that are bought tend to be made in Spain. This does not indicate a bias in the Spanish purchasing trend but merely indicates price and market availability.

Market penetration of household goods in quite poor considering the regional wealth differences. An example of this reflection is in the number of stoves bought *per capita*, which is less than the number, again *per capita*, bought in Portugal. However, consumer spend penetration is growing.

The breakdown of the household spend on goods and services is found on page 169.

Financial awareness

The Spanish are one of the lowest banked countries in the Community with only 34 per cent of the population having bank

Table 16.4   Household spend in Spain

Items	%
Furniture (including carpets and other floor coverings)	37
White goods	13
Furnishings	8
Table utensils	14
Domestic and other household services	28

Source   Eurostat/Mintel

accounts. There is also a low usage of other financial products at all levels. However, market penetration of credit cards is as high as in the UK.

The lack of use of different savings and investments is reflected by the spend priority given by the Spanish; research indicates that they would select as a priority holidays, cars or a second home.

Food spend

The Spanish consume more meat *per capita* than the British although over the last ten years this trend has slowed down. Pork and poultry are the preferred choices.

Despite being a sizeable wine producing nation, the Spanish preference is for beer which is drunk more than wine. Interestingly, Spanish consumers have one of the highest levels of desire in wanting a wider choice of alcohol-free drinks. This also reflects the consumers' desire to increase the availability of additive-free and low fat foods.

General consumer spend

The Spanish desire for clothes is low on the priority spend scale, indeed, the Spanish spend is almost the same as the Greeks and Portuguese.

Political trends

The Spanish have six political parties to consider when casting their Euro vote. Out of a total of 60 Euro seats, the Socialists still held on to power retaining 27 out of the 28 at the last Euro election.

The percentage of voter turnout in Spain is 55 per cent, just below the EC average of 59 per cent.

Green issues in Spain did not attract as much voter awareness as, say, in Italy.

ESTABLISHING A BUSINESS

Authorisation for investments by private investors from abroad are generally not required. However, the investment does require prior verification as a control measure by the Department of Foreign Transactions (DGTE) for the following types of investment:

1. The acquisition of more than 50 per cent of the capital of a Spanish company.
2. The formation of branches or establishments.
3. In certain cases, the acquisition of real property by foreign individuals not resident in Spain, and the acquisiton of real property by a legal entity.

Special rules apply to certain sectors of the economy, for example telecommunications, banking, defence and air transport.

The most common ways for a foreign investor to operate in Spain are through a joint venture, a branch or a subsidiary company. A minimum of three shareholders (acting on their own behalf or on the behalf of other companies or individuals) are required to form an SA company (*Sociedad Anomina*). There is no minimum or maximum capital requirement to form an SA company and ownership can be by a variety of shares.

For a *Sociedad de Responsabilidad Limitada* (SRL), the capital is divided into participations which are equal in value and are indivisible. The number of members cannot exceed 50 and the maximum capitalisation of an SRL is Pts 50,000,000.

Management structure

In an SRL, the company is represented by an administrator who need not be a shareholder, and the company may only have one administrator. No auditors are required for an SRL.

In an SA, the company is governed by a Board of Directors, or by a sole director. If there is a board, then three directors are required. As with an SRL, no auditors are required by law unless the company is listed on the Stock Exchange, or is a bank. However, the articles can require the appointment of auditors. Currently, there are no employee participation requirements.

SINGLE-MARKET EFFORTS

Government

A number of seminars have been held to discuss the Single Market, and it is a common theme of political speeches and major news articles. There is as yet, however, no co-ordinated Single

Market campaign. Moreover, no official surveys have been conducted.

USEFUL ADDRESSES

Sources of information and help
Spanish Chamber of Commerce
5 Cavendish Square
London W1M ODP
Tel: 01-637 9061

British Chamber of Commerce in Spain
Calle Marques de Valdeiglesias 3
E-28004
Madrid 4
Tel: (+34) 1 521 9622
Tlx: 45522 COBE E

Research sources
Instituto Dym SA (subsidiary of AGB Research)
Corcega 329 4a
E-08037 Barcelona
Tel: (+34) 3 2374480
Tlx: 50872 DYM E

Addresses for advertisers
Asociacion General de Empresas de Publicidad
   (advertising agents group)
Gran Via 57
Madrid
Tel: (+34) 1 2499458

Chambers of Commerce
Barcelona   Ample 11
              Barcelona
              Tel: (+34) 3 302 3366

Bilbao   Rodriquez Arias 6
              Bilbao
              Tel: (+34) 4 423 8546

Madrid   Plaza de la Independencia 1
             Madrid
             Tel: (+34)1 232 1011

Principal Euro Info centres

Centro Europeo de Informacion
Av Diagonal 403 ir
E-08008 Barcelona
Tel: (+34) 3217 20 08

Centro Europeo de Informacion
Alameda de Recaldo 50
E-48008 Bilbao (Vizcaya)
Tel: (+34)4 4444 054

Centro Europeo de Informacion
Diego de Leon 50
E-28006 Madrid
Tel: (+34) 1262 44 10

Centro Europeo de Informacion
Avda San Fransisco Javier s/n
Edificio Sevilla 2–9a Planta
E-41005 Seville
Tel: (+34) 54 65 04 11

17
THE UNITED KINGDOM

INTRODUCTION

The business culture within Britain is rapidly evolving from the days of rigid social and educational hierarchies to one of a more entrepreneurial environment. This process has been championed by Thatcherite policies and initiatives. It would be wrong, however, particularly in the City of London, to assume that ability, drive and ambition have yet overtaken the traditional social advantages of belonging to the 'right family' (old money), having a public school education (fee paying), and going to the right university, namely Oxford or Cambridge.

The UK is socially and economically split between the Midlands, the North, Scotland, Northern Ireland and Wales (collectively called The North if you speak to a southerner) where the country's light and heavy engineering industries exist, and the generally more affluent South, where service industries predominate. A line drawn on a map from Bristol to Norwich would approximate this imaginary divide.

In all business transactions with Britons, punctuality, initial formality, politeness, sincerity and a good grasp of the English language are essential.

MAKING THE APPOINTMENT

British business still retains quite rigid, self-important power hierachies. Many British managers will not admit to their limitations in the decision-making process and, although often speaking with convincing authority, they may have little real influence over the business decision. The most effective way of ascertaining the right person to contact is by writing direct to the owner of a small company, or to the 'Chief Executive', 'Managing Director' or 'Chairman' of a large company. In some companies, one person will hold two or three of these titles, so a telephone call to his secretary would identify his preferred form of address.

The decision-making body within medium or large British companies is normally the company's Board of Directors. Membership of this Board will be sought by most ambitious managers, and carries the title 'Director'. In most companies, the function of the individual director will precede the title, eg 'Sales Director', 'Operations Director', 'Finance Director', etc. Directors always outrank managers, with the exception of a General Manager, who will run a whole division, factory or major store for a company, and who will usually have directors reporting to him.

Differences in status are highlighted on business cards, which are generally offered more frequently the lower the status of the contact. This does not apply to guests offering their own cards; however, cards are used less frequently now than in the past.

The formality of British business would support initial contact through a well-written, appropriately addressed, well-researched letter. Men should be addressed as 'Mr' unless they have a title such as 'Sir', or 'Lord'. Women should be addressed as 'Mrs' if married, 'Miss' if single and 'Ms' if their marital status is unknown or if this is the preferred form of address. It is always better to address your letter to a named person within an organisation, and it should conclude 'Yours sincerely', with your own name and position underneath your signature. If you are really unable to find out the name of the person you wish to contact and do not know the sex of that person, never begin a letter 'Dear Sir or Madam'. Use 'Dear Sir' and conclude with 'Yours faithfully'.

Once you are on first name terms with your contact, it is perfectly acceptable to open a letter with 'Dear John', but note that it would be taken as a withdrawal of friendship to revert to surnames once first names have been used.

Following up the letter with a telephone call after an appropriate time is acceptable, and it is always a good idea to make friends with your contact's secretary. Time spent in building up a relationship with her will assist in getting your name into the decision-maker's diary (often controlled by the secretary). Do not assume that being offered an appointment with someone other than the initial contact is a slight. Interest has been shown and the correct communication channels defined for you.

Where it is likely that your business is unknown to the target company, it is useful to send corporate information beforehand, although do not be surprised if you get the impression that it has been read immediately prior to your meeting. This is, indeed, quite possible; the British are not famed for their preparation.

THE MEETING

It is unlikely that anyone other than those needed to discuss the proposal will be invited to the meeting by the British host, and he will almost certainly hold the meeting in his own offices. The discussion will usually begin and close with social conversation and the business discussion will be conducted with great politeness. However, it would be most unusual for minutes to be taken and a brief letter from you summarising the discussion is often advisable. This will serve to confirm any action you are about to take as a result of your discussions and can help to avoid decisions being reversed after the meeting. Some British managers are, unfortunately, apt to change their minds and be far less decisive after the meeting than during it.

The timing of the initial or subsequent appointments will indicate the appropriateness of entertainment.

ENTERTAINING

Business meals

Although the most ambitious British manager will start work at around 8.00–8.30 am (earlier if his factory is open) and finish around 6.30–7.00 pm, he has not yet quite taken to breakfast meetings. These are appropriate if taken *en route* to another meeting (say, on a train) or if you are staying at the same hotel overnight.

If a meeting is arranged close to noon, a lunch invitation will be given. If it is not forthcoming at the first meeting, however, this is not a negative indication. Either party can offer lunch, but the visitor should give the host ample time to suggest it. Business lunches are at least 50 per cent social, and serious business is often left until the coffee is served. It would be unusual for papers to be exchanged or referred to at the luncheon table. Aperitifs and wine are usual with the meal, which will normally take upwards of 90 minutes. If the invitation to lunch is yours, the British host can be offered the choice of restaurant, or you may choose it yourself. It is generally safest to stick to English or French cuisine, but, if you are planning something more exotic, check with you host's secretary whether he is likely to enjoy your choice.

The person offering the invitation usually pays the bill, although some British managers may insist on paying. It is wise to give in gracefully, after a short debate.

Business dinners are offered less frequently than lunches, and tend to be more friendly affairs. The same rules apply as to lunch, although business is even less likely to be discussed openly. The issue can be introduced, but should be dropped if the host seems unenthusiastic.

British business people tend to leave work between 5.00 and 6.00 pm, and take large amounts of work home with them. However, this desire to be home does not mean that an invitation to drinks after normal office hours will not be accepted. They are generally prepared to take business telephone calls out of hours once they offer their home number, but these should always be made in the early evening, and not later than 9.30 pm. Most business people will be unavailable during their two- or three-week family summer holiday, usually taken during the school vacation from late July to early September.

The British are prepared more than most to offer invitations to their homes. Although the acceptance to these is not a must, they do indicate a desire to build a positive relationship, and should be accepted if possible. It is appropriate to take a small gift of flowers, wine or chocolates, and a short note of thanks should be sent the following day.

Subjects for social discussion

Yes	No
Children	Politics
Headline news	War
Climate	Religion
Problems with the journey	Education
Sport	
Cars, houses and estates	

Business hospitality

Away from the business stage, business entertaining (designed to develop personal as well as business advantage) is common in Britain. The events offered vary greatly and may cover occasions where the host is the sponsor of the event to those which have particular importance to the British. These fall into two categories: the first being events where scarcity of tickets indicates the standing of the host company (eg Centre Court tickets for Wimbledon, Wembley Cup Final, etc), and second events at which it is socially advantageous to be seen (eg Ascot, Henley and Glyndebourne). Declining an invitation (backed, of course, by the appropriate excuses) is unlikely to cause major offence but business opportunities beyond the immediate may be lost, since such events often provide a wealth of contacts for the future.

It is unlikely that you will be in any way compromised by accepting such invitations and, even when a dinner invitation turns into a trip to a night-club, the British sense of propriety is generally evident.

Invitations may be offered to you alone, but where cultural evening events are proposed then the invitation will almost invariably include your spouse or partner.

The visitor is not expected to reciprocate, but a return invitation will usually be accepted. Care needs to be taken, though, to ensure that good faith is not lost. For instance, it is not wise to invite a more senior member of the organisation than you are dealing with instead of your contact, but it is good form to let him know of the invitation and gain his implicit acceptance.

Gifts

Business gifts are a part of business life between supplier and retailer, buyer and seller. In fact, around Christmas time business gifts are as expected as Christmas cards. The value of such gifts varies enormously, but is usually calculated so that it neither offends nor could be construed as a bribe.

Dress

In all business meetings it is best to dress in a fairly traditional manner. This means dark-coloured lounge suits for men (black, dark blue or grey), plain or striped shirts, good quality ties in non-garish colours and polished black shoes. For women, more colour can be introduced, but dress should not be flamboyant. A man is still judged by his appearance: brown shoes, nylon shirts or matching tie, shirt and handkerchief can definitely create the 'wrong' initial impression.

Invitations to cocktail parties or more formal occasions will usually indicate dress requirements: for example, 'black tie' (dinner jacket and black bow tie) and long dresses for ladies, or 'lounge suits' and 'cocktail dresses' for less formal affairs.

WOMEN IN BUSINESS

Few women outside the service industries hold senior jobs. Attitudes to women tend to vary with a man's age and past experience. Prejudice, where it exists, usually takes the form of condescension.

WORKING HOURS AND PUBLIC HOLIDAYS

The average working week is from 9.00 am to 5.30 pm, Monday to Friday. In industry, these hours may vary, often starting and finishing earlier than offices.

On average, Britons have four weeks' annual holiday. They will usually take two to three weeks in the summer, plus some extra time around Christmas. There is an increasing trend of taking winter sports holidays.

Public holidays are:

1st January	(New Year's Day)
	(Scotland one day longer)
1st Monday in May	(May Day)
Last Monday in May	(Spring Bank Holiday)
Last Monday in August	(August Bank Holiday)
25th December	(Christmas Day)
26th December	(Boxing Day)

In addition, there are two movable days, Good Friday and Easter Monday.

LETTER-WRITING

The envelope

To a man:	Mr (initials, surname), or (initials, surname) Esq[a]
To a married woman:	Mrs (initials, surname), or Ms[b] (initials, surname)
To an unmarried woman:	Miss (initials, surname), or Ms[b] (initials, surname

Salutation

To a man:	Dear Mr (surname)
To a married woman:	Dear Mrs/Ms (surname)
To an unmarried woman:	Dear Miss/Ms (surname
To an unnamed person:	Dear Sir, Madam
To a company:	Dear Sirs

Closing

| To a named individual: | Yours sincerely |
| To an unnamed individual or company | Yours faithfully |

Notes

[a] Formerly used as a mark of respect, particulary for proprietors of companies. Now rarely used.

[b] The title 'Ms' can be used where the woman's marital status is unknown, or where this is the preferred form of address. It is widely used by women in business.

MARKETING

The British economy has experienced a massive change in direction and focus since 1979. The introduction of free-market practices backed by monetarist economic policies and a *laissez-faire* political attitude have altered many of the country's business practices. However, advertising spending is still seen by business as a potential short-term route to protect the 'bottom line'.

The classification of consumers purchasing trends for marketing purposes into identifiable sectors has formed the cornerstone of most promotional strategies. The most common and basic classification is 'socio-economic grading'. Within this system there are five soci-economic grades:

Table 17.1   Socio-economic grading in the UK

Social grade	Percentage of population	Social status	Head of household's occupation
A	3	Upper middle class	Higher managerial, administrative or professional
B	10	Middle class	Intermediate managerial, administrative or professional
C$_1$	24	Lower middle class	Supervisory or clerical, and junior managerial administrative or professional

Social grade	Percentage of population	Social status	Head of household's occupation
C₂	30	Skilled working class	Skilled manual workers
D	25	Working class	Semi-skilled and unskilled manual workers
E	8	Lowest levels of subsistence	State pensioners or widows (no other earner) casual or lowest grade worker

Source JICNARS (Joint Industry Committee for National Readership Surveys)

More sophisticated life-style classifications are available, based on attributes other than occupation which give more meaningful and usable data. The initial classification of this type was developed by CACI Market Analysis and is called ACORN.

The split in the advertising pound in the media is approximately as follows:

Table 17.2   Media spend in the UK

	%
Press	61
TV	32
Poster and transport	4
Cinema	1
Radio	2

Source   MEAL (Meal Expenditure Analysis Ltd)

Media

VAT at 15 per cent is payable on all production and media costs for TV, outdoor, cinema and radio advertising. A levy of 0.1 per cent of gross media costs for press (except classified lineage and semi-display), outdoor, cinema and direct mail is applied to fund the Advertising Standards Authority (ASA). A special code of practice for sales promotion is in operation under the supervision of the ASA. No advertising for cigarettes is allowed on TV, nor in cinemas showing children's programmes. Spirits' advertising is not banned on TV by the government, but Independent Television (ITV) companies do not accept spirits' advertising: this is in keeping with their voluntary control system. Alcoholic drinks advertising may not be shown within, or around, programmes for children, or between 4.00 and 6.00 pm on weekdays. There are many restrictions for other advertising on TV, radio and in the press. For more information contact: The Independent Broadcasting Authority (IBA), 70 Brompton Road, London SW3 1EY (Tel: 01-584 7011); and Advertising Standards Authority, Brook House, Torrington Place, London WC1E 7HN (Tel: 01-580 5555).

The UK national daily press is divided between the serious press which covers business, and the popular press which does not (at least not seriously). The key papers for business are the *Financial Times*, followed by *The Times*, *Daily Telegraph*, *Independent* and *Guardian*. Sunday papers which cover business are the *Observer*, *Sunday Telegraph* and *Sunday Times*. There are a number of magazines which are published weekly and monthly: *The Economist*, *Investor's Chronicle* and *Financial Weekly* appear weekly and *Management Today* appears monthly.

The spend rankings by key categories are:

Table 17.3   Key categories in spending in the UK

		£m
(1)	Food	5.1
(2)	Retail, mail order	4.1
(3)	Financial	3.5
(4)	Automotive	3.2
(5)	Drink	2.0
(6)	Household stores	1.8
(7)	Toiletries, cosmetics	1.7
(8)	Leisure equipment	1.5
(9)	Holidays, transport	1.4
(10)	Household appliances	1.1

Source   MEAL

CONSUMER PREFERENCES/DIFFERENCES

Household spend

The British have the highest ownership in the EC of leisure electrical appliances, this can be seen in the volume of purchase in videos and homecomputers which ranks the highest in EC, and on purchase of stero equipment which ranks second to Germany. Indeed, despite the present Government's desire to see these imported goods reduced, the consumer spend on these items is still continuing.

In the overall spend on home furnishings, the British, like the Spanish, are middle-ranking spenders but when compared to Northern EC countries Britain is at the bottom of the furnishings league spend table. Interestingly, the spend on white goods, ie towels, sheets, blankets etc is high.

The breakdown of the household spend on goods and services is as follows.

Table 17.4   Household spend in the UK

Items	%
Furniture (including carpets and other floor coverings)	29
White goods	25
Furnishings	9
Table utensils	13
Domestic and other household services	24

Source   Eurostat/Mintel

Financial awareness

With Britain currently seen as the financial centre of Europe, it is not surprising to learn that the British are well banked, with a greater percentage of the population holding both a building society and a personal bank account. But if a central bank of Europe should be located in Germany then this will no doubt affect the volume of business in the future.

Britain (like France and Germany) tends to follow consumer trend patterns from the US, as can be seen in the penetration of credit cards which is one of the highest in the EC.

Food spend

Only the Germans and the Belgians drink more beer than the British. In other liquid consumption there has been a marked increase in the purchase of both mineral water and wine. The British, without doubt, drink more tea (both bagged and loose) than any other country in the Community.

Food spend levels on biscuits and chocolate are the highest in the EC, with many international companies trying to win its share of the confectionary market in the UK.

More milk is consumed in Britain than elsewhere and sales of other dairy products are high. Health awareness is growing and this is shown in a reduction in the consumption of food with a high fat content. British cheese is having a revival, especially farm-produced, although cheese import from EC countries is high.

Interestingly, in Britain the consumption of meat, poultry and fish differs from region to region with the West Midlands consuming more meat than the South East or North West.

Over the last decade, the British have become more used to eating out or buying take-away foods.

Hypermarkets and supermarkets are widely used although a recent trend shows that consumers desire a return to the 'high street' type of shop with its old fashioned, sometimes Victorian, appearance.

General consumer trends

Britain ranks third in the purchase of passenger cars although unlike France and Italy, there is no home-brand loyalty.

The British are gradually becoming more aware of green issues with recent surveys showing that the consumer will pay more for environmentally-friendly products. The British car industry, however, has yet to match the environmentally-friendly Germans.

Political trends

Environmental issues played an important role for the first time in the British electorates' opinion. Although the Green Party had over 2 million votes cast, no UK Green MEPs hold a seat as Britain still has not adopted proportional representation.

Britain is the bottom of the league table in voter turnout showing a mere 36 per cent.

Out of 81 Euro seats, the Labour Party gained 13 seats more than the Conservative Party (Labour 45, Conservative 32).

ESTABLISHING A BUSINESS

No permission is required to establish a business presence in the UK and there are no exchange controls. A foreign corporation may establish either a subsidiary or a branch in the United Kingdom. Most foreign companies set up a local private company (*Ltd*) rather than a public limited company (*Plc*). No consents are needed; no local shareholders or directors are required; minimum capital of £100 issued shares apply to companies. Capital duty (1 per cent) is due on shares issued; certain documents (for example, memorandum and articles of association) have to be filed. A foreign corporation which sets up a UK branch must, within 30 days, register certain documents (with an English translation) and appoint a local representative.

Management structure

In the UK, the features of public and private companies are not as distinct as they are in other European countries. There are no minimum capital requirements for the registration of a private company, and shares can be issued in different classes. The company acts through directors, and those whom they appoint to run the company.

A private company must have at least one director, who can be the shareholder, and a company secretary. The company secretary acts as the chief administrative officer. Non-executive directors are not employed by the company and have no individual power as directors to bind the company in business, other than as a member of the board.

In public limited companies (plc), the company will usually have, in addition to its main board, a management committee. The main board will consist of both executive and non-executive directors, who will usually be appointed by the Chairman. The link between management and board is the Managing Director or Chief Executive. A Company Secretary in a public company must have the relevant company secretarial qualifications. Otherwise, apart from a minimum authorised capital of £50,000, the structure is the same as for a private company, or 'close' company (five directors or less).

Audited accounts must be filed each year with Companies House based in Cardiff. In addition, accounts have to be filed with the Inland Revenue. Sole traders or partnerships need only file accounts with the Inland Revenue.

There are no formal worker participation requirements for UK companies, and no legal requirements for worker councils, although relationships with trades unions are emerging from a phase of economic co-operation.

Businesses can also be conducted through a partnership or as a sole trader, in which case the income is taxed in the hands of the individual or the partners, whichever is applicable.

SINGLE-MARKET EFFORTS

Government

A campaign was launched in 1988 which was co-ordinated through the DTI. It featured press, television and radio advertisements backed by an information pack, regularly updated. Details are shown in Table 4.1 on page 44. A DTI database has also been set up, together with various other skill centres.

Business

A series of industrial breakfast presentations were organised around the UK. Chambers of Commerce and trade associations are making active attempts to keep companies up to date with information and advice.

USEFUL ADDRESSES

Sources of information and help

Association of British Chambers of Commerce
212 Shaftesbury Avenue
London WC2H 8EB
Tel: 01-240 5831

Research sources

A.C. Nielsen (all Nielsen's European operations are
  co-ordinated from this office)
Nielsen House
London Road
Headington
Oxford OX3 9RX
Tel: 0865 742742
Tlx: 83136

Market Research Society
175 Oxford Street
London W1
Tel: 01-439 2585

Addresses for advertisers

Advertising Standards Authority
Brook House
Torrington Place
London WC1E 7HN
Tel: 01-580 5555
Fax: 01-631 3051

Independent Broadcasting Authority
70 Brompton Road
London SW3 1EY
Tel: 01-584 7011

Institute of Marketing
Moor Hall
Cookham
Berks SL6 9QH
Tel: 06285 24922

Institute of Practitioners in Advertising
44 Belgrave Square
London SW1
Tel: 01-235 7020

Chambers of Commerce

Aberdeen   15 Union Terrace
Aberdeen AB9 1HS
Tel: 0224 64122

Belfast   22 Great Victoria Street
Belfast BT2 7BJ
Tel: 0232 244113

Birmingham   PO Box 360
75 Harborne Road
Birmingham B15 3DH
Tel: 021-454 6171

Bristol   Clifton Park
Bristol BS8 3BY
Tel: 0272 737373

Cardiff   101–108 The Exchange
Mount Stuart Square
Cardiff CF1 6RD
Tel: 0222 481648

Edinburgh   3 Randolph Crescent
Edinburgh EH3 7UD
Tel: 031-225 5851

Glasgow   30 George Square
Glasgow G2 1EQ
Tel: 041-204 2121

London   69 Cannon Street
London EC4
Tel: 01-248 4444

Manchester   56 Oxford Street
                 Manchester M60 7HJ
                 Tel: 061-236 3210

Principle Euro Info Centres
Euro Info Centre
8 Storey's Gate
London SW1P 3AT
Tel: 01-222 8122

Euro Info Centre
4 Cathedral Road
Cardiff CF1 9JG
Tel: 0222 371631

Euro Info Centre
Windsor House
9–15 Bedford Street
Belfast BT2 7EG
Tel: 0232 40708

Euro Info Centre
7 Alva Street
Edinburgh EH2 4PH
Tel: 031-225 2058

18
WEST GERMANY

INTRODUCTION

The stereotyping of West Germany (Federal Republic of Germany) as efficient, conscientious and formal is to a large extent relative. In reality, Germany is not a cold nation controlled by the formality of its culture. Germans respond positively and creatively within a framework well known and understood. The crux of successful business relationships is reading the hidden agenda while responding to the surface normality.

The more Calvinistic North (Hamburg, Bremen and Hanover) tends to reflect the ethos of hard work and there is a serious attitude to life. Many people, particularly the elderly, maintain that the country has strayed into a more relaxed, lazier state, and there is some truth in this. Germany's workforce do put in fewer working hours than they once did: 20 per cent less in just over 15 years. On average, their working week is 20 per cent shorter than the Japanese, and they have longer holidays than the British. However, although there may have been a quantitative decrease, there is no sign of a qualitative deficiency. Work is tightly focused, with little time spent socialising and time-filling. This quality expectation is obvious in all aspects of business life, from the initial interview where small talk is seen as just that, to expectations of behaviour in business partners.

Germans are, however, surprisingly accommodating to the 'frailty' of other nations, provided, that is, they make adequate efforts. Germans, who have one of the highest levels of dual-language competency at board level in Europe, are able and willing to discuss business in a foreign language if they are proficient in it. However, in any such conversation you should always acknowledge the effort that the German is making and you should respond appropriately, by talking more slowly than usual, using fewer idioms and at all times being patient and polite.

To achieve business success in the German market you need

to be very good at what you do, and maintain your achievement. If, for instance, your advantage is based upon technical superiority then should that be lost, so will the business.

Germans are accomplished and demanding commercial negotiators. They will require excellent business references, demonstrations of products, and evidence of some well-researched information as to their business needs.

The German's national prejudice towards other nations will also figure in the type of terms required in any deal. For British firms, tight delivery dates, high penalties for failure and generous warranty periods will usually be included in any contract. However, given satisfactory performance, a German client will pay on time and keep to the letter and spirit of any agreement.

MAKING THE APPOINTMENT

Formality is the key to a successful business relationship. It begins with establishing a rapport with the executive's secretary. (German secretaries really do see themselves as an extension of their bosses, and expect formality in all matters.) The initial contact is best received in a well written, personally-addressed letter. Because of the hierarchical nature of the German business culture, a letter addressed to a level senior to the one with whom you are likely to transact the contract will, if passed down, enhance the receptivity of the German negotiator.

The letter should be written in good business German. A poorly constructed letter will work against you. You should, when writing, use the impersonal address *Herr* or for women, married or single, *Frau*. Responses to letters should take about two weeks, after which a telephone enquiry is acceptable. If you are unable to speak German, the letter seeking a personal interview (Germans will expect to meet personally to conclude any serious business transactions) should state this, and you should offer to bring an interpreter to the meeting. If your German host wishes to use his languages, or if such an interpreting facility is available within the company, he will let you know.

Formality in the conduct of the meeting is as important as it is in the letter. You should avoid being late or, come to that, early. A German's diary is full, and an early arrival can be as disruptive as a late one. Expect everything to be arranged. Everyone, from the receptionist upwards, will know you are coming. Your visits will be arranged with great efficiency, but the pace may seem extremely slow.

THE MEETING

Be well prepared for the first, usually quite short, meeting. Your German counterpart will act as 'host'. Business-orientated opening comments (for example, 'you have a fine factory') are expected as small talk, not personal enquiries. It is polite and sensible to follow the lead of your host, responding to his speed, level of detail, and direction. To be seen to be uncomfortable or irritated at the rate of progress or level of detail would offend one of the unwritten rules. If you are using your own language, make sure you choose your words carefully, using simple linguistic constructions so as to flatter your host's skill in front of his junior colleagues.

It is possible that lunch will be offered, but notification of this will probably have been given before the meeting. If you have issued the invitation, you will be expected to pay.

One of the most striking elements of a German business meeting is the hand shaking which takes place. This occurs on every possible occasion, at the beginning and close of meetings and extends to everyone joining the meeting, and leaving midway through (although unexpected interruptions are unlikely to occur).

ENTERTAINING

Business meals

In Germany, business meals will almost exclusively be lunch or dinner, although German business people will start before the core business time of 9.00 am to 5.00 pm, or match industrial times. German style is to start work early, and meetings at 8.30 am are common, although banks (a major influence on business) are likely to keep meetings until after 9 o'clock in the morning. Lunch is likely to be taken early: 12.00–12.30 pm, and hardly ever will the meal commence after 1.00 pm. Alcohol is acceptable, but the extended business lunch has lost favour now. A simple pre-lunch drink and wine is the general rule.

Most middle to senior managers will be willing to accept lunch, although members of the *Vorstand* (management board) may decline. Lunch is unlikely to take more than 90 minutes and more usually will last just one hour. Dinner or pre-dinner drinks at a German's home are an important sign of progression both in terms of business and personal relationships. In most cases, restaurant dinners are normal for quite a while in the relationship.

If visiting a German's house either for drinks or dinner, it is important to take flowers for the lady of the house. This custom is well known to German florists, who will construct an appropriate arrangement. A gift of wine, in addition, is becoming more common if you are dining at your German host's home, particularly if this is seen as part of your own tradition.

Although it is right and proper to shake the hand of your host, your hostess's hand should only be taken if extended. In German company, those well known to the hostess might kiss her extended hand; however, you should not do this until you know her well. It is expected that a few days after dinner you will send a brief 'Thank you' note.

Toasts at formal dinners are very short. The host will say just a few words of welcome, to which all those dining will respond by thanking him. If required, your response should be short and simple.

The Germans have a very close-knit business and social community. To break in to this takes time and patience; never to do so is common. An understanding of German culture, art and literature helps. The major corporations are still run by some of Germany's oldest money and by the banks. Deutsche Bank, for instance, is the largest bank and the largest shareholder in the largest company, Daimler-Benz. Banks and their attitude to investment, solid, low-risk attitudes, shape the philosophy of most companies.

Subjects for social discussion

Germans are well read and have a good understanding of world affairs. Education, environmental and individual development are issues for discussion. In many cases, the understanding that you should 'never mention the war' is likely to be pre-empted by it cropping up in your German host's conversation!

Business hospitality

Business hospitality is nowhere near as extravagant as in, say, the UK or France. Formal hospitality events are rare, and the Germans are unlikely to organise them outside working hours.

Gifts

These are welcome, provided they are seen as just that. A logoed pen, business folder or diary are acceptable, but expensive gifts cause embarrassment and are unwelcome.

Dress

Formality in dress, accompanied by overt cleanliness, is important on all occasions. Men wear plain suits, not necessarily dark, and white or blue shirts either plain or with a discrete stripe. Coloured shirts with white collars are accepted as 'British' but flamboyant ties and boldly striped shirts are viewed with suspicion. Clean shoes are also important, regardless of the weather conditions.

WOMEN IN BUSINESS

Only about 2 per cent of the major companies have women at senior levels. Those women who hold senior positions have usually inherited them from husbands or fathers, or have started the business themselves. This chauvinistic attitude to women is projected on to foreigners. Although a German business man will be polite, he is likely to believe that the business woman is acting on behalf of a male colleague who will be consulted prior to any agreement being reached.

WORKING HOURS AND PUBLIC HOLIDAYS

The core business hours are 9.00 am–5.00 pm, although many executives will start as early as 8.00 am and finish after 6.00 pm. Germans have, on average, five weeks holiday, of which three to four are likely to be taken in summer, during July and August.
   Public holdidays are:

lst January	(New Year's Day)
6th January	(Epiphany)
1st May	(Labour Day)
17th June	(National Unity Day)
15th August	(Assumption)
1st November	(All Saint's Day)
25th/26th December	(Christmas Day)

There are, in addition, six movable days, including Easter.

LETTER-WRITING

The envelope

German	English
Herr (initials[a], surname)	Mr
Frau (initials[a], surname)	Mrs
Fraulein (initials[a], surname)	Miss

Salutation

If the letter is written in:	
German	English

German	English
Sehr geehrter Herr (surname)	Dear Mr (surname)
Sehr geehrte Frau (surname)	Dear Mrs (surname)
Serh geehrtes Fraulein (surname)	Dear Miss (surname)
Not used	Dear Sir
Sehr geehrte Damen und Herren	Dear Sirs

Closing
Individual: Mit freundlichen Grüssen Yours sincerely
Company: Hochachtungsvoll   Yours faithfully

Note
[a] The first forename may be used instead of the initial.

MARKETING

Germany's development as a marketing economic force is based upon four major facts:

1. social market economy;
2. membership of the EC;
3. anatomy of the *Bundesbank* and free money and capital movements;
4. accord between the trade unions and employers.

(This almost creates a national corporation: Government, unions and employers.)

These factors have led to an economy with a steady inflation rate, level unemployment and a controllable growth in GNP. In this environment advertising and media opportunities have grown. It is estimated by *Gasaintverbank Werkeagenturers* (GWA), the joint Advertising Agency Associations, that by the year 2000 the gross income of advertising agencies will triple from the 1985 figure, to DM 49.9 billion, which is just under DM 1,000 for each of the population.

Unlike the UK, there are no fixed socio-economic groups for marketing purposes. Target groups are defined in terms of sex, age, education, region, size of household and children in household. However, for purposes of defining an upper class (AB),

German marketers usually use the following classification: household net minimum income of DM 3,000 a month, and head of household's educational level of at least High School graduation.

The split of advertising DM in the media is approximately as follows:

Table 18.1   Media spend in West Germany

	%
Newspapers	28
Consumer magazines	38
Trade magazines	5
Television	16
Radio	7
Outdoor	5
(Media)	1

Source   Nielsen

The spend rankings by key categories are:

Table 18.2   Key categories spend in West Germany

(1)	Travel, tourism
(2)	Cosmetics, pharmaceuticals
(3)	Food
(4)	Beverages (alcoholic and non-alcoholic)
(5)	Banks, insurance
(6)	Household cleaners
(7)	Clothing, textiles
(8)	Tobacco
(9)	Furniture

Source   Nielsen

Media

There are no specific advertising taxes: VAT is charged at 14 per cent. Prescription drugs are not allowed to be advertised on any medium. Tobacco advertisements are not permitted on TV or radio. There are restrictions on the advertising of alcoholic beverages and on advertising aimed at children, or advertising which uses children. For further information, contact: Deutscher Werberat, ZAW, Postfach 200647, 5300 Bonn (Tel: 228 351025).

CONSUMER PREFERENCES/DIFFERENCES

Household spend

Germany is the EC's biggest consumer spender. The Germans 'spend total' on their purchase of goods (homes, clothes, etc) is more than any other EC nation. On home appliances, the Germans have the highest penetration of electrical goods except for stereos, where they are second to the UK, and leisure electrical goods. For example, there are more dishwashers, electric stoves and central heating systems sold in Germany than elsewhere in the Community.

The breakdown of the spend on household goods and services is as follows.

Table 18.3   Household spend in West Germany

Items	%
Furniture (including carpets and other floor coverings)	29
White goods	25
Furnishings	9
Table utensils	13
Domestic and other household services	24

Source   Eurostat/Mintel

Financial awareness

In common with most of Northern Europe, the Germans have a high penetration of bank usage. However, they prefer to pay cash for their purchases and so the level of penetration of credit cards is low. Being a consumer-hungry society, the volume of cash transaction is considerable, and supports a high technology trend in store equipment.

Over the last few years the Germans have taken the financial lead in Europe which could culminate in the European Central Bank being situated in their country.

The Germans are not as well served with other financial

products as the British but are well ahead of their neighbours in the Netherlands.

Food spend

The Germans top the league table in the consumption of beverages drinking more beer, orange juice and coffee, and are second only to the Belgians in their consumption of mineral water. They drink more spirits than elsewhere in the Community.

The preference for meat products is high, roughly equal amounts of fresh and tinned are sold. Pork is their favourite meat and there are many varied products.

General consumer spend

More cars are bought in Germany than elsewhere and the same is true of bicycles.

The Germans are environmentally-aware, with consumer selections of 'green' products taking priority over others. The Germans tend to be more health conscious but this is seen not necessarily in the reduction of their fat and drink intake but more in the preference for physical exercise.

Political trends

The swing to the right in West Germany can be seen by the Republican Party gaining six seats. The green vote remained steady, gaining one further seat.

Voter participation in Germany is above the EC average showing a turnout of 62 per cent.

ESTABLISHING A BUSINESS

Every new enterprise must report its intention to commence business to the local economic supervisory office (*Wirtschafts und Ordnungsamt*) in the municipality concerned, which will issue a certificate of registration (*Gwerbeanmeldeschein*). Some industries (for example, food, pharmaceutical and medical products, banks, insurance companies and transport) require special licences. Proof of the qualifications or reliability of those concerned must be produced; without such proof, an examination conducted by a Chamber of Commerce or other body must be passed.

Every new business must register with the Commercial Register (*Handelsregister*) maintained at the local court, the municipal trade tax office (*Stadtsteueramt*), the local tax office (*Finanzamt*), and (as soon as employees are engaged) the local social security office (*Allgemeine Ortskrankenkasse*). It must also join the Chamber of Commerce in the area in which its head office is situated. Any enterprise in which a non-resident makes an investment, whether by partial or complete acquisition or (in many cases) by way of a loan, must report the investment to the Federal Reserve Bank through the appropriate state central bank, unless it is only DM 20,000 or less in any year.

Building permits are required for the construction of new buildings. In some industries a special licence may be required to construct or occupy particular types of industrial buildings.

There are two types of limited liability company; the private *Gesellschaft mit beschränkter Haftung* (GmbH), and the public limited, *Aktiengesellschaft* (AG). AGs are set up by large, corporate enterprises who wish for large scale public participation. Small to middle-sized businesses would find it difficult to make the administrative and financial outlays to comply with the Company's Act. The minimum capitalisation of a GmbH is DM 50,000, whereas an AG requires DM 100,000. Although both types of company issue share certificates, this is not a requirement for a GmbH.

Management structure

The business of a limited liability company is conducted by one or more managing directors (*Geschäftsführer*), who need not be German nationals or residents, nor need they be members. In an AG, this is done by the Board of Directors (*Vorstand*). Among other duties, the managers are responsible for maintaining the company's statutory records and for the preparation of financial statements. An individual manager's power to bind the company in transactions with third parties, however, cannot be effectively limited, except by requiring joint signatures – either of two managers or of one manager and a managing employee (*Prokurst*). Managers are personally liable to the company and its members for any damage caused by unauthorised acts. They are also liable to fines or imprisonment if they fail to declare a bankruptcy within three weeks of learning that the company is insolvent, and the company continues to incur liability. A non-resident manager should appoint a resident deputy who will be answerable to the authorities for the proper conduct of the company.

A public or private limited liability company is required to have a supervisory board (*Aufsichtsrat*), in addition to a board of managers, if the number of its employees regularly exceeds 500. A smaller company may provide for a supervisory board in its articles of association, if it so wishes. If the supervisory board is a mandatory one, one-third of the members must be elected by the employees, the other two-thirds being elected by the shareholders. If there are more than 2,000 employees, one-half of the members must be elected by the employees and the supervisory board must appoint a labour director or personnel manager (*Arbeitsdirektor*) to the board of managers. In situations where a compromise seems unlikely, the chairman, elected either by a two-thirds vote of the board or by the shareholders' board members alone, has a casting vote. The function of a supervisory board is to oversee the company's activities. It may also be required to give prior approval to major decisions taken by the managers. Members of the board need not be German nationals or residents.

Employees of a company with more than five employees have the right to establish a works council (*Betriebsrat*). This consists of elected representatives of all the employees. The functions of a works council include the consideration of social, personnel and economic policies. Its approval is required for decisions affecting employment, such as mergers, plant relocations or changes in production methods. A company with over 100 employees must also set up an 'economic committee' (*Wirtschaftsausschuss*). Such a committee comprises a small number of management and employee representatives with the right to receive and discuss periodic information on sales, production and financial matters. The committee is consultative only and does not have the power to approve or disapprove of activities.

SINGLE-MARKET EFFORTS

Government

An information booklet was produced by the Federal Economic Ministry in July 1989.

The first meeting of the National Conference on Europe took place on 7 December 1988, bringing together business men, trade unions and professional bodies to discuss the Single Market and their place in it. The conference was addressed by Chancellor Kohl. It was decided that these meetings should take place regularly every six months.

Business

Chambers of Commerce are providing members with a wide range of information on the Single Market. Large business (for example, Deutsche Bank) are also organising seminars on 1992.

Surveys

A survey conducted by the IFO Institute in Munich suggests that 52 per cent of companies expect to benefit greatly from the Single Market. Interestingly, only 7 per cent of those interviewed thought that they would suffer from its introduction.

USEFUL ADDRESSES

Sources of information and help

*Austellungs – und Messe – Ausschuss der
    Deutschen Wirtschaft AG* (Confederation
    of German Trade Fair and Exhibition
    Industries)
Lindenstrasse 8,
D-5000 Koln 1
Tel: (+49) 221 209070

British Chamber of Commerce in Germany
The Secretariat
Heumarkt 14
D-5000 Cologne 1
Tel: (49) 221 234284
Tlx: 8883400 FIBLD

*British Marketing Office (Advanced
    Technology)*
Kron Prinzstrasse 14
7000 Stuttgart 1
Tel: (+49) 711 294562
Tlx: 722 397
Fax: 0711 229271

Bundesverband den Deutschen Industrie (BDI),
    (Federation of German Industry)
Gustar-Heinemann-Upr 84–88
Postfach 510548
D-5000 Koln 51
Tel: (+49) 221 370800

Deutscher Industrie – und Handelsrag (DHIT)
    (Federation of German Chambers of Commerce)
Abernaveneralle 148
D-5300 Bonn 1

*German Chamber of Industry and Commerce
    in the UK*
12–13 Suffolk Street
London SW1Y 4HG
Tel: 01-930 7251
Tlx: 919442 GERMAN G

Research sources

A. C. Nielsen Company
PO Box 160531
Ludwig Laudmann Strasse 405
D-6000 Frankfurt am Main 16
West Germany
Tel: (+49) 69 79380
Tlx: 412031

ADM-Arbeulsbneiss Deutscher
  Markforschungsin (Market Research
  Association)
Burgschmeitstrasse 2
85500 Nuremberg
Tel: (+49) 0911 395 231

Addresses for advertisers

Gesellschaft Werbeagenturen (West German
  advertising agencies body)
Friedenstrasse 11
D-6000 Frankfurt am Main
Tel: (+49) 69 235096

Interessengemeinschaft Deutscher Fachmessen
  und Austellungsstadte (Trade Fair organisers)
Margaretenstrasse 4
D 7000 Stuttgart 60
Tel: (+49) 711 335629

Chambers of Commerce

Berlin   Hardenbergstrasse 16–18
                  Berlin 12
                  Tel: (+49) 30 31801

Bonn   Bonner Talweg 17
                  Bonn
                  Tel: (+49) 228 22840

Bremen   Am Markt 13
                  Bremen
                  Tel: (+49) 421 36371

Cologne   Unter Sachsenhausen 10–26
                  Cologne 1
                  Tel: (+49) 221 16401

Dortmund	Märkische Strasse 120 Dortmund Tel: (+49) 231 54171
Dusseldorf	Ernst-Schneider-Platz 1 Dusseldorf Tel: (+49) 211 35371
Frankfurt	Börensplatz Frankfurt Tel: (+49) 69 21971
Hamburg	Adolphsplatz 1 Hamburg 11 Tel: (+49) 40 361380
Hanover	Berliner Allee 25 Hanover Tel: (+49) 511 31071)
Munich	Max-Josephastrasse 2 Munich Tel: (+49) 89 51161
Nuremberg	Hauptmarkt 25 Nuremberg Tel: (+49) 811 20591
Stuttgart	Jägerstrasse 30 Stuttgart Tel: (+49) 711 20051

Principle Euro Info Centres

EG-Beratungsstelle für Unternehmen
Dohne 54
D-4330 Mulheim Ruhr
Tel: (+49) 208 300 04 31

EG-Beratungsstelle für Unternehmen
Helwigstrasse 33
D-2000 Hamburg 20
Tel: (+49) 40 460 20 87

EG-Beratungsstelle für Unternehmen
Adenauer Allee 148
Postfach 1446
D-5300 Bonn 1
Tel: (+49) 228 10 40

EG-Beratungsstelle für Unternehmen
D. Martin Luther Strasse 12
Postfach 110 355
D-8400 Regensburg
Tel: (+49) 941 569 41

INDEX

INDEX OF ADVERTISERS